AF706398

ANTONIO FAJARDO NAVARRO

# Connected, but with common sense

*A practical guide for parents, adolescents, and teachers to protect their digital identity and reputation*

*Copyright © 2025 by Antonio Fajardo Navarro*

*All rights reserved. No part of this publication may be reproduced, stored or transmitted in any form or by any means, electronic, mechanical, photocopying, recording, scanning, or otherwise without written permission from the publisher. It is illegal to copy this book, post it to a website, or distribute it by any other means without permission.*

*First edition*

*This book was professionally typeset on Reedsy.*
*Find out more at reedsy.com*

# Contents

# 1

# Author introduction

My name online is **CrookedSpaniard**, a pseudonym I have been using for years across social media, educational projects and the occasional late-night technological experiment that was, in hindsight, not particularly wise. It is a name that has taken on a life of its own: it appears in my podcasts, my courses, conversations with students... and, according to my children, on far more screens than would be considered socially acceptable.

We live in a fascinating, and slightly exhausting time, where our **digital image and digital footprint** can be almost as valuable as our ID card... and, if we are being honest, sometimes even more so. There was a time when you could have a bad day, embarrass yourself and trust that nobody would remember. Now you embarrass yourself and **your bad day comes with 4K resolution, automatic subtitles and an algorithm ready to push it on TikTok**.

This book is the result of a mixture of experiences: working as a teacher, leading innovation projects, being a parent and remaining, permanently, a student of the digital world. Over the years, I have seen the very best and the very worst of online behaviour, from incredibly creative teenagers who build impressive digital identities, to others who learn (sometimes the hard way) that posting something "just for friends" is not always quite as "just for friends" as it sounds.

And right in the middle of all this are **families and teachers**, trying to accompany without invading, guide without overwhelming and protect without switching into *"CSI: Parental Edition"* mode.

If you worry about the safety, reputation or digital future of your children or students... if you have ever thought, *"What if what they post today affects them tomorrow?"* or if you simply want to understand this world without losing your sanity, then this book is for you. If you are a teenager, you can read it too, seriously.

Here you will find:

- Clear explanations, without unnecessary technical jargon.
- Humour (because without humour, the Internet becomes a very long place).
- Practical advice you can use both at home and in the classroom.
- Real examples that may feel uncomfortably familiar.
- And one central idea: building a positive digital footprint **is possible**... and **accompanying that process is too**.

You do not need to be an expert in social media, to have had a Tuenti account (RIP), or to know exactly what an algorithm is. You only need something you already have: the willingness to understand and to help.

So take a breath, keep an open mind (like Neo in The

Matrix… you have to watch the film) and get ready to look at the digital world with different eyes. Ideally, your own… not your neighbour's, who also happens to have Instagram.

You will come across definitions and concepts throughout the book that may feel familiar, repeated, or make you think, "this again." This is not a mistake. I can be a bit persistent, and I genuinely believe these ideas are worth repeating. My apologies in advance.

# 2

# The digital world we live in: a modern survival guide

## Welcome to the digital jungle

(Not especially dangerous, but definitely a bit chaotic)

If someone had said back in the 1990s that one day we would be able to send photos of our dinner to thousands of people in a second, order food without speaking to another human being, or that your fridge might recommend recipes, we would probably have thought they were exaggerating. And yet, here we are, living somewhere between science fiction and everyday routine.

The digital world has infiltrated absolutely everything: school, work, communication, relationships, leisure, hobbies… and even the way we argue (and make up afterwards). But the most interesting part is not how much we use technology, but **how often we use it without even realising it**.

This chapter is a basic map to understand the terrain. It is not meant to scare anyone or demonise screens. I promise: there will be no alarmist speeches, no "back in my day" lectures, and no excessive nostalgia for indestructible Nokias. Well… maybe a *tiny* bit of nostalgia, but strictly for scientific reasons.

Let's begin.

## Why doesn't the Internet come with instructions?

There are everyday objects—like a simple stapler—that come with twenty-page safety manuals, complete with diagrams. And yet the Internet, which can change a life for better or worse in a matter of minutes, arrives with **no instructions at all**. No leaflet. No warnings. No helpful "do not put your fingers here" label. Nothing.

And still, there is no official guide explaining:

- When it is a good idea to post something (spoiler: rarely when you are very angry),
- What you can share without regrets,
- What you should **never** share, not even if your best friend insists,
- How to interpret a comment without automatically assuming everyone hates you,
- When to be suspicious (short answer: more often than you think),
- And how all of this quietly shapes your real identity, even though you never asked it to.

Most of us were thrown into the digital pool with a phrase that really should come with a very large asterisk:

*"It's very intuitive, you'll see."*

An asterisk that, of course, nobody ever explains. Because yes, it is intuitive, until three new icons appear, a menu mysteriously moves, a button that was never there suddenly exists, and you find yourself questioning your basic life skills.

Teenagers grow up in this environment like fish in water, that's true. But that does not mean they know how to swim properly. Many are simply floating as best they can. And adults... well, we perform impressive juggling acts between notifications, pop-up windows and the eternal question: *"Where did I save that?"*, a sentence that really should come pre-installed on every phone owned by someone over thirty.

In short: **The Internet did not come with instructions.**, so this book aims, with all due humility, to be the user manual that never arrived in the box.

## Connected life: light, shadows and screens

The Internet is a wonderful place... and also one capable of producing existential headaches.

Let's start with the bright side, explained in a bit more detail so it does not sound like a technology brochure:

- **Unlimited access to information.** This sounds fantastic until you realise that "unlimited" means exactly that. You look for a simple omelette recipe and end up reading about how beavers build houses. The Internet is a gigantic library, open 24/7 and with no librarian telling you to be quiet, but you need filtering skills to avoid getting completely lost.
- **Creativity without limits.** In the past, being creative required cardboard, felt-tip pens and an adult willing to buy more cardboard because you cut it wrong. Now, a phone is enough. Teenagers compose music, edit videos, design, draw, code and invent trends, sometimes without leaving the sofa. It is a wonderful creative explosion, although it can also create the feeling that *"if I don't create something every day, I am nobody."*

- **New forms of friendship.** Social networks have expanded the idea of making friends. You can now have a best friend in another city, a group that shares your favourite niche obsession, or a community that understands you better than your entire class. Of course, this also means learning the difference between genuine friendship and *"this user interacts with me because the algorithm says so."*
- **Dynamic learning.** If a teenager wants to learn to play the ukulele, fix a bike or understand maths, they can do it immediately. Not when term starts. Not when someone has time. Right now. The Internet is an endless academy where teachers never sleep and tutorials last exactly as long as your patience.
- **Incredible opportunities.** From building an artistic portfolio to meeting someone who can open doors, the Internet is a factory of opportunities. That said, finding them requires learning to ignore all the fake doors that appear first.

And now, the shadows, explained with a little more honesty and digital realism:

- **Constant comparison.** No matter how well things are going, there will always be someone who has travelled more, has better lighting in their photos or has just achieved something incredible while you are still in pyjamas eating cereal. The Internet is a shop window where everyone shows their best side, and we compare our behind-the-scenes with everyone else's highlights. A terrible combination.
- **Social pressure.** Likes, comments, followers, best friends

lists, posting rhythm... Teenagers often feel there is an invisible rulebook dictating how they should behave online. Nobody knows who wrote it, but everyone seems convinced it exists.

- **Disinformation at supersonic speed.** Rumours used to take days to spread; now they take thirty seconds and a retweet. False information travels faster than real information because it is usually more exciting. It is the digital version of "my friend's cousin said so": quick, easy and dangerously convincing.
- **Privacy risks.** Every click, every permission and every "accept all because I'm in a hurry" leaves a door open. Nothing happens... until something does. It is like turning on lights at home without checking whether you have left a window open.
- **The classic "I just came to watch one video and now two hours have passed."** Time behaves differently online. Five minutes on the Internet equals a full expedition through the algorithm. It is the closest thing to a daily black hole: you enter watching one video and come out wondering whether it is still the same day.

Nothing is entirely good or entirely bad. The Internet is a tool, and like any tool, everything depends on how we use it.

A hammer can build a house, or smash a thumb.

Same tool.

Exactly the same thing happens with the digital world.

## What do teenagers actually do online?

A common question among families:

*"What are they doing in there for so long?"*

Short answer: living.

Long answer: it depends on the day, their mood, the algorithm and the Wi-Fi.

Common activities include:

- Maintaining friendships (yes, whatsapp counts),
- Expressing emotions they may struggle to verbalise offline,
- Searching for community: gamers, dancers, artists…
- Learning things that are not taught at school,
- Disconnecting from stress,
- Experimenting with identity,
- Following trends they swear they are not following,
- Laughing at absurd videos (a universal activity).

And yes, procrastinating… although let's put it more clearly. Procrastination is postponing something you know you should be doing now, but which mysteriously loses all appeal the moment it needs to be done. It is not pure laziness; it is more a mix of "I don't feel like it now" and "I'll definitely feel like it later", even though later never quite arrives.

Teenagers have simply transferred this skill into the digital realm: replacing a task with a video, a message, a meme or an absolutely essential search such as *"how to organise my life in five easy steps"*. And if there were Olympic Games for procrastination, adults would still hold the lifetime achievement gold medal, but teenagers would fight hard for silver with tutorials, sudden motivation and, of course, a video explaining why they will start tomorrow.

For them, the Internet is not "a tool", but a fully social space. A place where they relate, comment, argue, joke, create, reconcile and, occasionally, do homework. It is the main meeting point of their generation.

It is the new school playground: less concrete, more pixels. Instead of wooden benches and goalposts, there are group chats, private accounts, shared memes and conversations that start at eight in the morning and end... well, technically they never end.

And like any playground, there are laughs, misunderstandings, shared secrets, inside jokes and the occasional situation that becomes more complicated than necessary. The difference is that this playground does not close when the bell rings, and what happens there does not always stay there.

That is why understanding it, and accompanying young people within it, is so important for families and teachers.

## Technology, family and living together: finding balance

Digital coexistence can generate more arguments than choosing a film to watch together.

Classic examples:

- "Just five more minutes, I promise."
- "But all my friends are allowed to do it!"
- "I'm not addicted, I just... need it."
- "I swear I'm in class, Mum." (while the camera is mysteriously off)

They may sound like everyday dinner-table phrases, but each hides a small philosophical battle between generations. Teenagers fight for digital autonomy; adults fight to preserve the little sense of control they still have.

Balance does exist, although it requires practice and more patience than assembling furniture without instructions. Some important realities, explained with a touch of humour, because otherwise we might cry:

1. **Teenagers do not want to miss out.** FOMO (search in Google… or ChatGPT if you don't know what it is ☺) - is not a mythical creature; it is real, strong and well-fed by constant notifications. For them, disconnecting for five minutes feels like disappearing from the planet.
2. **Adults do not want to lose control.** And sometimes we confuse accompanying with monitoring. We want to know what is happening, who they talk to, whether they are safe… without turning into MI6 agents. The challenge is being present without invading.
3. **Everyone needs limits.** Teenagers, adults and even phones, which after sixteen hours switched on have the same energy as an office worker on a Friday afternoon. Limits are not punishments; they are barriers that stop the digital river from sweeping us away.

The goal is not to turn the home into a military base where every notification needs written permission. It is to build reasonable digital habits: habits that allow conversation without shouting, agreements without drama and negotiation without emotional blackmail.

In short: digital coexistence is not easy, but with common

sense, humour and honest conversations, peace is possible... even with Wi-Fi.

## Small mental tools for better navigation

Here are simple ideas that work like small digital superpowers:

The three-second pause

Before posting, commenting or replying, take a moment. Three seconds. Not deep meditation, just enough time to ask yourself: *"Does this represent me?"*

If the answer is unclear, if you feel a tiny doubt, or if your brain makes that internal "hmm... not sure" noise, it is probably better not to post. What we write in a rush is usually what we regret the most later.

The trusted adult test

Imagine the people who mysteriously activate our common sense: a teacher, a future boss, a grandparent or your future self (the one who hopefully sleeps more and makes better decisions).

If you picture raised eyebrows or a silent *"oh dear"*, it may be time to rethink.

The balance rule

If online life starts taking up more space than real life, like adding too much salt to food, it is time to readjust. Not to reject the digital world, but to stop it from swallowing important moments

This is not about giving up digital technology or living in a cave without Wi-Fi, but about avoiding screens taking over important moments: real conversations, proper rest, meals without notifications, or even the simple ability to be bored for a while (an underrated but very useful activity for the brain).

"Do I need this, or am I just doing it out of habit?"

Many of us open apps like we open the fridge when we are not hungry: out of inertia. Asking this question breaks autopilot.

Asking yourself "do I really need this?" is not meant to be a deep philosophical reflection, but a way to break autopilot mode. Sometimes you realise you didn't actually want to open that app at all, your brain was just looking for a quick hit of stimulation. Other times, you genuinely did want to open it, and that's fine. The key is that it's a choice, not a reflex.

The most liberating idea

You do not need to be everywhere, follow everything or give your opinion on every trending topic. You do not need to post everything you live.

The Internet will still be there tomorrow. You can rest. You can disappear for a few hours. The digital world does not get offended. And if someone does… they probably need a break too.

## Section for teachers: practical classroom ideas

Here are realistic, useful ideas—even for chaotic days:

### *Mapping digital use*

Ask students to write down all the ways they use the internet: social, academic, creative, recreational… even the ones they say "don't count" (they do). Then, as a group, analyse it as if you were digital archaeologists: which uses add something positive, which are neutral, and which create stress or mental noise without offering much in return? The key is for them to discover for themselves what adds value and what takes it away, rather than giving them a ready-made list.

*Debate: "Internet, angel or villain?"*

Students often split into two camps from the very first minute: "the internet is the best thing in the world" versus "the internet destroys lives". The aim is not for one side to win, but for them to understand that a tool can be both things at the same time. Use real-life examples: situations where the internet has been incredibly helpful, and others where it has complicated someone's life in a completely unnecessary way. The discussion becomes much more engaging when they realise that almost everyone has experienced moments of both.

*Real screen analysis*

Ask them to keep a voluntary record of their screen time during a normal day. A special Sunday doesn't count, nor does the day they decide to behave themselves. Then, analyse the results together. Which activities take up the most time? What surprises them? What will they passionately try to justify? This activity often leads to funny and very revealing conversations: many realise they spend more time "just having a quick look" than on activities they genuinely enjoy.

*Digital empathy activity*

Ask the group: "What things make you feel good online? And what makes you feel bad?" Although it may seem like a simple question, it opens up a whole world: comparisons, pressure to reply instantly, fear of missing out, but also humour, support and creativity. It's a fantastic way for them to listen to each other and realise they are not the only ones who feel the way they do.

### *Create a group digital code*

Suggest that they create a digital coexistence code for the group: respect, breaks, privacy, asking for permission before recording or sharing... Rules work far better when they come from the students themselves rather than from a poster on the wall. The fun part is seeing how they agree on what they consider reasonable and what they see as over the top. When they design it themselves, they follow it with more conviction and fewer complaints.

## Welcome to the journey

The digital world is neither a monster nor a permanent theme park, even if at times it has more unexpected twists than a rollercoaster and more lights than a fairground. Nor is it a villain trying to trap us, or an ideal paradise where everything works perfectly. It is simply a complex, vast and slightly unpredictable ecosystem in which all of us, teenagers, families and teachers, are learning as we go, improvising more than we care to admit, and moving forward with a mix of intuition, experience and the occasional mistake.

The good news is that we are not alone on this journey. No one has absolute control over the digital world, and anyone who claims they do has probably not updated their privacy settings since 2014. What really matters is understanding that navigating this environment does not require perfection, but curiosity, common sense and a touch of humour to survive those moments when technology seems to have a mind of its own.

This chapter has sketched out the overall map: a broad overview, a compass to help us find our bearings, and a reminder that there is no need to master everything straight away. The next chapters will help you go deeper, better understand each part of the journey and, above all, feel that yes, it is possible to live in this digital world without getting lost… or at least knowing how to find your way again when Google Maps decides to stop recalculating.

# 3

# Digital footprint: the trail we leave without remembering we passed through

A digital footprint is like that memory box we all have at home… but with a twist.

It does not only contain photos from the time when we all had a questionable fringe in 2007. It also includes every action, search, click and digital slip-up we make on the internet. And the best, or worst, part is that this box is not stored under your bed, but scattered across platforms, apps, services, companies, websites and algorithms that remember more than your grandmother remembers the list of her grandchildren.

Many families think that a digital footprint is simply "what you post". If only it were that easy. That is just the visible part of the iceberg. The huge, cold and slightly dangerous part lies underneath: what you do not post but is still recorded. From how long you take to swipe past a video to how many times you search "how to delete browsing history quickly".

Get ready. We are going to take it all apart using humour,

real examples and very clear explanations.

What is a digital footprint really?

In short, **everything we do online leaves a trace.**

That trace can be voluntary, such as uploading a photo, or involuntary, such as accepting cookies without reading a single word because the banner covers half the screen and you just want to see the croquette recipe already.

The digital footprint is divided into two main types.

## Active digital footprint

This is the footprint we leave on purpose, with intention, more or less thought through:

- Uploading a photo.
- Commenting on a video.
- Creating your seventh account because you can no longer remember the passwords to the previous six.
- Liking a meme that represents you on a deeply personal level.

### *Everyday example*

Your daughter uploads a photo with the caption:

"It's so hot today." It sounds innocent enough, doesn't it? But a stranger replies: "Which city do you live in?" and she answers without thinking.

She has just shared her location, climate, routine and even possible schedules, without meaning to.

And just like that, an innocent comment turns into a weather update with free geolocation included.

### *More fun (and very real) examples*

- You upload a photo of your dog and the internet works out your neighbourhood from the park in the background.
- You comment "I'm starving" and suddenly you see adverts

for sushi, kebabs and kitchen robots.
- You like three craft videos and the algorithms decide you are now a professional artisan.

The active footprint is the visible part, but the passive footprint is the one that really makes people nervous.

## Passive digital footprint

This is the footprint you leave **without even realising** it. Yes, even when you are not posting anything at all. It is like leaving digital breadcrumbs everywhere, but without that conscious moment of thinking "I'm going to drop a breadcrumb here". It just happens. Your phone, your apps, your social networks and even your browser collect information about you as if they were motion sensors, always alert, always awake and definitely always hungry for data.

It includes:

- Cookies that record the pages you visit, because websites behave like that nosy neighbour who always wants to know where you have been.
- Apps that store your location because they "need it to function", even if it is just a torch app.
- Services that analyse how long it takes you to close a video. If you stay half a second longer, you are classified as "a person potentially interested in similar content forever".
- Platforms that know your preferences better than your own family. They know what time you log in, what colours you like, what content you consume when you are tired and what you watch when you want total escapism.

In short, **the passive digital footprint is that silent trail you leave even when you say nothing online**. Ironically, it is often the most complete, detailed and valuable trail for platforms. It is the digital version of "I'm not doing anything... but everyone is watching".

*Realistic example*

You search "how to make croquettes" once.

In less than 24 hours, your phone seems to have decided your culinary destiny:

- Adverts for kitchen robots.
- Recommendations for Japanese cooking courses.
- Air fryer tutorials.
- And, if you are unlucky, an offer for a master's degree in gastronomy.

That is passive digital footprint in action. You do one thing and the internet decides it is now your personality.

*Another example*

You spend three seconds longer than usual watching a cat video.

Result:

- TikTok wants you to adopt three cats.
- Instagram suggests veterinary accounts.
- YouTube recommends "How to know if your cat is judging you (spoiler: yes)".

## Why does the digital footprint matter?

Because the digital footprint **does not disappear**.

It has no expiry date.

It does not vanish like 24-hour stories.

It cannot be erased with CTRL plus Z.

Most importantly, **it builds the image that others have of us**, even before they meet us.

Why is this so important?

Because every click, search, comment and photo adds points to a kind of invisible CV that represents you wherever you go. Even if you do not remember it, the internet does. It is like that friend who remembers every embarrassing story perfectly, multiplied by ten and available globally.

Think of the digital footprint as a digital version of yourself living online and collecting all your online decisions. Sometimes that version looks charming and professional. Other times, well... it has photos with questionable filters, impulsive comments and searches you would rather forget.

And here comes the funny, or tragic, part. **People usually meet that digital version before they meet you**. Your "real self" arrives after your "digital self" has already spoken. And while you can explain, justify or clarify your decisions, that online version cannot. It speaks for you without consulting you.

That is why understanding and looking after your digital footprint is not about paranoia. It is about strategy. It is about making sure that the parallel version of you living online works in your favour, not against you.

*Example*

A teenager applies for a place at a top university. Everything goes perfectly… until a teacher searches their name on Google.

A video appears of them at 13 taking part in the "Exploding Watermelon Challenge".

Does it ruin their life? No.

Does it help? Not really.

Is it funny? Very.

But it stays there, as part of their digital trail.

## Clear examples to understand it better

### *Example 1: The innocent comment that never died*

Marcos, aged 14, writes on a gaming forum:

"My teacher is so annoying, I wish he would mute."

He laughs, closes the forum and forgets about it.

Years later, while looking for work experience, **that comment appears indexed on Google.**

The interviewer happens to be a fan of the same game.

Plot twist: it was not funny.

*Example 2: The browsing history that follows you like it has a life of its own*

You search "how to fix a tap".

For weeks, your phone thinks you live surrounded by leaks:

- Home insurance adverts,
- Plumbing tools,
- Renovation companies.

A friend looks at your screen and thinks you are restoring a cathedral.

*Example 3: Grandma's desserts in obsessive mode*

Your daughter searches for sweet recipes for a month.

TikTok concludes that her destiny is to become a professional pastry chef. Basketball is irrelevant. The apps have spoken.

Result: her digital footprint says "elite-level baking".

What should families know?

1. **Nothing truly disappears**. Even if you delete a photo, someone may already have saved it. And not just someone. It may also be stored on a server, in an automatic backup or in a copy you did not even know existed. The internet has an elephant's memory, but one that takes supplements. Everything we upload has the potential to outlive our intentions.
2. **Algorithms learn fast.** Sometimes too fast. With just

a couple of clicks, they can deduce more about us than a relative at Christmas dinner. If a teenager watches two sports videos, the algorithm decides they now live, breathe and dream sport. If they search for a book, they are recommended the entire bookshop, without checking whether it was genuine interest or just homework.

3. **What we share reveals more than we imagine.** A simple photo can show much more than a nice face. Location, time, lifestyle, friendships and routines can all be revealed. Even small background details can tell part of the story. Without realising it, we build a very complete digital portrait.
4. **The digital footprint affects the future.**Universities, companies and even future friends can see the image you have been creating. This is not to scare anyone, but to remind us that your digital version often arrives before you do.
5. **The digital footprint can also be positive.** Fortunately, building a good online image is easier than it seems. A creative project, a blog, a portfolio or respectful participation in a community all add up. The digital footprint is not only a risk. It is also a brilliant opportunity to show who you really are.

## Practical advice for guiding without scaring

### *1. Talk as a family about what is shared and what is not*

No CSI-style interrogations. The idea is conversation:

- What do you like posting?

- How do you choose what to upload?
- Who can see it?

Do it while cooking, walking or having a snack. Sit down, do not judge and ask with curiosity.

*2. Review privacy settings together*

Once a term. Like changing the bed sheets.

No drama required. Simply:

- Check public versus private profiles,
- Decide who can comment,
- Look at which apps have access to the camera.

*3. Teach the "this could be saved" principle*

A magic sentence:

"If you wouldn't say it in front of your grandparents, think twice before posting it."

It works surprisingly well.

*4. Lead by example, even when it hurts*

Adults leave digital footprints too, and sometimes very questionable ones. That passive-aggressive comment you left on Facebook in 2011, that sepia-filtered photo of doubtful artistic quality, that "I'll look at it later" attitude towards privacy warnings... all of that represents you too.

Here is the important part. Your children observe everything. Not always to judge you, although sometimes they do, but because they learn from what they see. If you share without thinking, they will too. If you laugh at a borderline meme and then tell them to be careful, digital coherence quietly leaves the room.

Leading by example does not mean being perfect. It means being conscious. Say decisions out loud:

- "I'm going to check the privacy settings before posting this."
- "I'm deleting this comment because it adds nothing."
- "I'm going to check whether this news is real."

Your children do not need epic speeches. They need **to see you act the way you want them to act.**

### *5. Not everything is risk. The digital footprint can be very positive*

Among so many warnings, it is easy to forget that the digital footprint can also be **a powerful tool**. Not everything is danger, drama and technological catastrophe. There is also a bright side to the digital ecosystem.

A well-cared-for online trail can show:

- Creativity, such as drawings, music, videos or writing.
- Commitment, such as school projects, volunteering or achievements.
- Skills, such as presentations, tutorials or portfolios.
- Genuine interests, such as reading, sport or research topics.

And, believe it or not, **opportunities often come from**

**there**. A teacher discovering a student's blog, a school valuing consistency in a personal project, a future employer noticing respectful participation in forums.

The key is to understand that the digital footprint is not only what can get you into trouble. It can also **open doors** that would take years to open in the offline world.

So, it is not just about avoiding risks, but about building positive signals that show who you really are.

## Mini checklist for families

- Do I know which platforms my children use? (If you think Facebook, I have bad news...)
- Are their profiles public or private? (Key question: did your child decide, or did the app decide by default?)
- Do we review what they share together? (Not as Inspector Gadget, but as sofa companions with hot chocolate.)
- Do they understand risks without drama? (No "the internet will eat you", but also not "post whatever you want, who cares".)
- Do I help them build a positive digital image? (Encouraging projects, achievements and good ideas, not just memes and videos of their cat screaming.)
- Do they know which apps have access to their location? (Because some apps know where you are more often than your own mother.)
- Do they know when content defines them and when it does not? (Spoiler: a video dancing with a raccoon filter is not their true essence.)
- Have we ever talked about the image they want to project? (Responsible person with a future? Creative artist? Myste-

rious cloud photographer?)

## Extended suggestions for teachers in the classroom

### *1. Guided debate using real examples*

Bring two or three anonymised real cases related to digital footprint into the classroom: one positive, one neutral and one with unexpected consequences. For example:

- A student who created a science blog and gained followers and opportunities.
- A case where an impulsive comment caused a real conflict.
- A situation where an innocent piece of content was misinterpreted.

Ask students to analyse:

- Which part of the digital trail was positive?
- Which part was problematic?
- What decisions could have been taken differently?
- How does perception change depending on who views the content?

The key is helping them evaluate **intention** versus **impact**, which is fundamental when understanding digital footprint.

### *2. Practical activity: "Google a fictional character"*

Divide the class into groups and give them an invented name: "Lucía Torres Martínez", "Diego Campos Bernal", "Sofía Ríos Delgado".

The task is to build the fictional digital footprint of that person:

- Which networks would they use?
- What kind of comments would they leave?
- Would they post artistic, sporting or humorous content?
- What impression would a stranger get when searching their name?

Each group then presents their "investigation" as digital detectives.

This activity helps students understand that **what appears about us online is not always fully under our control, but we can influence it.**

### *3. Analysis exercise: "What message does this post send?"*

Show different posts generated by AI or taken from public sources: party photos, sarcastic comments, selfies, viral challenges, motivational quotes.

Then ask:

- What impression does this give if you are their friend?
- And if you are a teacher?
- And if you are a coach?
- And if you are someone who does not know them at all?

This helps students understand how **context changes interpretation**.

### *4. Critical thinking and algorithms*

Ask students to open the same app, TikTok, YouTube or Instagram, and compare their home pages.

They will discover that despite similar ages, interests and schools, their recommendations are completely different. This opens discussion about:

- How algorithms work.
- Why platforms do not show the same content to everyone.
- How our interactions shape our digital experience.
- The dangers of living inside an information bubble.

You can even draw a simple chart on the board showing the different content categories each student sees.

### *5. Positive online presence project*

Ask students to build a small positive digital presence. It could be:

- An artistic portfolio.
- An educational blog.
- A video explaining a skill.
- A mini documentary.
- A presentation about a personal interest.

Then analyse together:

- What does this content communicate?
- Is it professional, creative and respectful?
- Would it help this person in the future?
- What would you improve if you were their "digital manager"?

The aim is to help them understand that **their digital footprint can be a springboard, not just a risk.**

*6. Final reflection: "What do I want the world to know about me?"*

Invite students to write one sentence describing how they would like to be perceived online. For example:

- I want people to think I am creative.
- I want to show that I am responsible.
- I want to share what I am passionate about.
- I want people online to get a real sense of who I am.

Then ask them to review their social networks, or those of a fictional character if they prefer privacy, and list:

- Which content reflects that image?
- Which content does not fit?
- What could they publish to reinforce it?
- What should they archive or change?

This activity helps connect **intention** and **action**, which is crucial in building digital identity.

# 4

# Who am I online? Identity, reputation and posting history

The question "Who am I online?" sounds simple... until you start thinking about all the photos, likes, comments, videos, old accounts and posts that live in your little digital corner. At that point, the answer becomes more complicated than trying to close 87 browser tabs without losing the one you actually needed.

On the internet, our identity is not a single message or a profile picture. It is a mixture of decisions, big, small and microscopic, which together form the image others have of us. It is our "social avatar", but one we have not always designed on purpose.

And in the case of teenagers, that identity is being built while they are still trying to work out who they are away from the screen. A difficult mission, definitely expert mode.

This chapter aims to help families and teachers understand what shapes digital identity, how it affects reputation, what risks it involves and how to support young people so that their "digital self" is a little more aligned with their "real self", or at least does not go completely rogue.

What is digital identity?

Digital identity is the combination of **everything we do, show or allow to be seen online**: posts, comments, likes, friendships, personal style, consumption habits and even the things we do without realising it. Essentially, it is the sum of every small footprint we leave during our daily digital walks, even when we think no one is watching.

If we stop and think about it, digital identity works like a giant jigsaw puzzle. Each piece may seem insignificant on its own, but together they create a surprisingly accurate picture. What is fascinating, and sometimes unsettling, is that this picture forms even when we are not "posing". The internet draws us whether we notice or not.

In simple terms:

- What you upload becomes part of your identity. From the epic holiday photo to that meme that represented you a bit too well.
- What you do but do not upload, such as searches, likes or viewing time, also becomes part of it. Your clicks speak. Your silences do too.
- What others upload about you matters just as much, or even more. A badly chosen tag, an unexpected photo or someone else's comment can build parts of your identity without asking your permission.

We can imagine digital identity as a **biography written by several authors**: you, your friends, your favourite platforms and that algorithm that seems to know you better than your own father. In fact, if someone asked you what your favourite ice cream flavour was and you hesitated, TikTok would probably answer before you did.

The most curious thing is that this biography is not stored neatly in a nice book on a shelf. It is scattered across servers, profiles, cookies, histories and corners of the internet that occasionally bring back things you did not even remember doing.

In short, **digital identity is the version of you that the internet sees, remembers and shares**, whether you like it or not. That is why understanding it is the first step towards having some control over it.

## Digital image vs digital identity

Although they are often used as if they were the same thing, digital image and digital identity are two different layers of our online presence. Understanding the difference is key if we do not want to confuse what we show with what we actually communicate.

**Digital image** is what anyone can perceive at first glance when they come across your online presence: your profile photo, your most recent posts, your bio, the style of content you share. It is a quick, superficial and highly editable version of you. It is, so to speak, your digital shop window. You can change it in seconds with a new photo or a clever sentence.

**Digital identity**, on the other hand, is the deep, accumulated set of everything you do online. Not only what you post, but also what you comment on, what you like, the searches you make, your usage patterns, how you interact with others and even what others post about you. While digital image is what you seem to be, digital identity is what you actually project, often without meaning to.

A useful way to understand this is to think about the difference between a beautifully designed book cover and the actual content of the book. The cover attracts attention, can be very polished and look great, but it does not always reflect what is inside. Digital identity is that internal content: more complex, longer-lasting and much harder to control.

*Extended example: A teenage girl uploads photos where she appears happy, sociable and confident. That is her digital image: bright, friendly, stylish and apparently balanced. But her digital identity tells another story. Searches related to anxiety, private messages asking for support, posts that she deletes ten minutes after uploading them. All of this forms part of her digital identity, even if no one else sees it.*

Another common case is a teenager who posts very little, has a neutral profile picture and whose digital image looks discreet. However, their digital identity includes hundreds of hours consuming certain types of content, active participation in specialised forums and interaction only with specific groups. The public image says "quiet person"; the deeper identity says "highly involved in specific communities".

This distinction matters because we often judge, or are judged, by digital image, while consequences, opportunities and risks come from digital identity. You can appear to be one thing while actually communicating something quite different.

**Digital image is the cover. Digital identity is the whole book, including the chapters you thought no one had read.**

## Online reputation: how it forms without us noticing

Online reputation is how others interpret your digital identity. It is like an unsolicited report that the internet writes about you and, to make matters worse, never asks you to proofread before sending it out into the world.

What is fascinating, and slightly unsettling, is that **your digital reputation is built even when you are not thinking about it**. You do not need to plan a big post or make a public mistake. Simply existing online is enough.

It feeds on small daily details, such as:

- A comment that seemed funny to you but sounded like a hidden criticism to someone else.
- Repeatedly liking controversial content, which for you is curiosity and for others looks like a clear position.
- Being tagged in photos where you are not exactly showing your best side.
- Responding impulsively in a debate, leaving behind a digital trace of a heated moment.

Here is the trick. **Digital reputation does not ask for context**. The internet does not know if you were in a bad mood, if you acted without thinking or if you were just trying to be funny. It only sees the result and adds it to the portrait it is building of you.

We can imagine it like a school rumour that no one knows who started, but which happily travels through the corridors. In the digital environment, the same thing happens. One isolated interaction can become part of your "online legend" without you even realising it.

The most curious part is that reputation forms both through what you do and what you seem to do. Sometimes a simple pattern, even a casual one, is enough for others to draw quick conclusions:

- If you always comment the same way, people think you are like that.
- If you never say anything, people think you are distant.
- If you only post happy photos, people think your life is

perfect.

- If you are not online, people think you do not exist, at least digitally.

In short, online reputation is the version of you created from digital breadcrumbs. A construct that does not always match who you really are, but which, like a well-fed rumour, can travel much further than the truth.

## Old posts: the digital past that never retires

Social networks have an excellent memory. Sometimes too excellent. If human memory worked in the same way, no one would ever embarrass themselves again at weddings, family dinners or birthdays with questionable karaoke. But while our minds select, forget or edit memories, the internet is more like an infinite filing cabinet with absolute faith that everything must be kept forever. Especially the things you would rather delete.

While you change, evolve, mature and redesign your style, the internet keeps that 2016 video where you were spinning around with a puppy filter. You have moved on. Unfortunately, the internet has not. For platforms, that video is still part of your essence, like a masterpiece that must be preserved.

This leads to the **usual problems**:

- Posts that no longer represent who the teenager is. What once seemed fun or brave now causes full-body cringe worthy of a teenage horror film.
- Impulsive comments written at the age of 13. Yes, the golden age of absolute opinions and poorly calibrated

sarcasm.

- Videos that seemed harmless but no longer fit. Especially those involving dances, absurd challenges or spontaneous performances you swear you never approved.
- Past trends you would now ask to be buried. Not just buried, but locked away in a safe, inside a bunker, at the center of a volcano.

All of this happens because the digital past **never retires**. It does not rest. It does not say "my work here is done". It simply waits, ready to be discovered by a new teacher, a recent friend or, worst of all, by the algorithm itself, which suddenly decides to revive that forgotten gem as if it were doing you a favour.

That is why it is so important to understand that old posts are not just memories. They are part of your active digital identity, even if they no longer represent you. And although we wish the internet would do what we do and selectively forget what makes us uncomfortable, its policy seems to be exactly the opposite.

**Reviewing, cleaning and updating profiles is essential**. Like cleaning out your wardrobe, except this time it actually helps. Because while your awful jumper from 2012 can stay hidden at the back of a drawer forever, your 2012 video does not have the same luck.

Doing this clean-up is an act of digital self-care. It allows your "current self" to speak louder than your "ten-years-ago self", the one who still thought uploading 25 photos from the same angle was a great idea. Ultimately, it is about making sure your digital past does not keep making decisions for you in the present.

## Focused real-life examples (for you, teenager)

### *1. The "it was just a joke" comment*

Nuria comments under a video:

"Wow, this guy is so annoying."

She sees it as humour. He sees it as an attack. Friends see it, comment on it and exaggerate it.

Result: her online reputation changes without Nuria even noticing.

### *2. The perfect life that is not so perfect*

Tomás uploads flawless photos, always calm, always perfect.

His followers think he lives in a perfume advert.

In reality, he is exhausted trying to maintain an image that does not always reflect his real life.

### *3. The group chat that escaped the group*

A private class group shares memes and harsh jokes. Someone takes a screenshot. That screenshot reaches a teacher.

Mystery solved. Privacy over.

### *4. The video without permission*

Claudia records a friend dancing and uploads it "only for close friends".

Someone forwards it. The friend gets angry.

Claudia learns that "close friends" does not always mean

"closed circle".

## The oversharing phenomenon

Oversharing happens when someone shares too much, too fast or without enough filtering.

Examples:

- Posting every intense emotion.
- Uploading 25 stories from the same moment.
- Announcing where you are, who you are with and at what time.
- Constantly seeking validation through posts.

Sometimes the best version of yourself is the one that takes a break from posting. Not a dramatic break announced with a mystical message like "I'm leaving, don't look for me", but a simple digital pause. Close the app, look up and remember that, surprisingly, the world keeps working even if you do not upload a story every thirty minutes.

In fact, taking that pause often brings wonderful results. It is like tidying your room and finding things you did not even know you had lost. By pausing the need to share everything, you discover that some emotions make more sense without being posted, that some photos are nicer when they stay in your camera roll and that some moments are better enjoyed when you are not thinking about filters.

Sometimes, disconnecting for a while turns you into your own best influencer. For yourself. No algorithms, no metrics, no pressure. Just you, your real life and the calm knowledge that you do not need to be constantly connected to be relevant.

## The screenshot effect

Universal principle:

If it can be captured, it can be shared.

Even if it disappears.

Even if it is private.

Even if it lasts 24 hours.

Total security does not exist.

That is why teaching people to think before posting is essential.

One impulsive message can turn into a long-term problem thanks to a single screenshot.

## Social comparison and digital pressure

Constant comparison causes:

- Stress
- Low self-esteem
- A distorted perception of reality

Teenagers compare their normal life with the filtered version of other people's lives. An unfair battle from the start. You are comparing your real day with someone else's "best day", with filters included.

## Public, private and semi-private profiles

- Public: more exposure, more care needed.
- Private: better, but not foolproof.
- Close friends or best friends: misleading sense of security.

Many problems happen precisely in these semi-private spaces, where the feeling of trust is too high.

## Practical advice for families

### *1. Regular digital check-ins*

Review profiles together from time to time. Not as digital police, but as support. No need for dark glasses and "we need to talk". Sitting on the sofa calmly and seeing what has accumulated is enough. It is like checking the fridge. There is always something you did not know was there, something slightly worrying and, with luck, something still usable.

### *2. Talk about what cannot be seen*

Likes, viewing time and patterns also communicate. Sometimes more than posts themselves. It is like reading between the lines, digital edition. Someone thinks they are only watching cooking videos "out of curiosity" and suddenly the algorithm has decided they want to be a professional chef. Talking about the invisible helps break the myth of "if I don't post, I leave no footprint". If only.

### *3. Use the "future me" rule*

"Would you like someone to see this in five years?"

It is a wonderful question because it works like an express time machine.

If the answer is a clear yes, go ahead.

If the answer is "well… it depends", think again.

If the answer is an internal scream saying "no, please", the decision is already made.

### *4. Help, do not invade*

Create a safe environment, not an interrogation. If you use an inspector's tone, you will get suspect-style answers. Genuine curiosity, on the other hand, makes it easier for them to share doubts, mistakes or worries. The idea is to accompany, not to carry out a full digital audit, tempting though that may be.

### *5. Reinforce the positive*

Celebrate projects, creative ideas and skills, not just pretty photos. If only aesthetic content is reinforced, it is easy for teenagers to think their digital value depends on likes rather than on what they can learn or create. Applauding a presentation, a drawing, an educational video or a personal project is worth far more than saying "you look cute" for the twentieth time.

## Practical advice for teenagers

Here are some tips that work like good WiFi: simple, useful and hopefully activated by more people.

**You do not have to impress anyone online.**

Really. Not even when you get that perfect front camera angle, which happens roughly once every solar eclipse. People forget other people's posts quickly, but you keep the pressure of maintaining an impossible character. The internet does not need another epic version of you. It needs your authentic version, or at least one that does not cost you tears or battery.

**Do not post when you are angry.**

And if you can avoid posting when you are hungry, tired or just after arguing with your parents, even better. Posting while angry is the digital equivalent of sending a message at 3 a.m. saying “I’m just being honest”. It rarely ends well. Breathe, go for a walk or eat something. Everything improves when you are not in volcano mode.

**Do not record or share anything without permission.**

This is not a recommendation. It is a universal law, like gravity. If you record without permission, you get into trouble. If you share without permission, you double that trouble. And if someone takes a screenshot, congratulations, it is now an eternal problem. Asking for permission does not make you less fun. It makes you less likely to be called into school the next day.

**Your reputation is built through consistency, not virality.**

A viral video gives you 48 hours of glory and sometimes 48 days of regret. People will remember how you behave day to day far more than a dance that almost made it into an advert. Being polite, respectful and coherent works infinitely better than any improvised choreography.

**If something makes you uncomfortable, ask for help.**

This includes strange messages, posts you are unsure whether to delete, groups that turn toxic or situations that “feel off”. Asking for help does not make you weak. It makes you smart. And it usually stops a small problem from turning into one of those situations worthy of a documentary.

## Final mini-checklist

A short list to help you look at your digital reflection without panicking.

**Does your profile reflect who you really are?**

Or does it reflect who you were three years ago, or who you thought you wanted to be for one week?

**Do you have old content that no longer represents you?**

If the answer is yes, relax. We all have a digital past we would happily lock in a safe.

**Do you know who can see what you post?**

And "my friends" is not an acceptable answer. Sometimes the audience includes friends, friends of friends, a distant cousin and a stranger who has spent three hours analysing your profile.

**Are you comparing yourself too much with others?**

Remember: you see your behind-the-scenes, and you see everyone else's highlight reel. Unfair comparison from the start.

**Could you explain your digital identity without feeling embarrassed?**

If your answer is "more or less", you are on the right track.

If your answer is "I'd rather not talk about it", it might be time for a digital clean-up.

## Suggestions for teachers

Here are some proposals designed to make students reflect without falling asleep, or at least not too much, and to help you work on digital identity without turning into a technological security guard.

### *1. Activity: "Three posts, three identities"*

Present three fictional posts and ask students to imagine what kind of person is behind each one. Then analyse together whether those conclusions were accurate or full of assumptions.

The aim is to help them understand that we judge very quickly online, sometimes too quickly, and that one post says far less than a whole person.

### *2. Workshop: "Redesign your digital identity"*

Ask students to create a mini positive portfolio. It can include a short text, an image, a video, a drawing or a class project. Then analyse together what it communicates.

The fun part is seeing how small decisions completely change external perception. It is like showing them that they have an "edit button" for their reputation.

### *3. Debate: "If you see it, do you share it... or not?"*

Perfect for discussing boundaries, consent and the eternal internet dilemma: "it's just a screenshot, what could happen?".

Spoiler: a lot. A lot a lot.

This conversation usually leads to very funny moments, especially when students realise that no, not everything that makes them laugh should be shared.

### *4. Practical privacy exercise*

Configure together who can tag them, see their posts or hide old content. A kind of digital MOT, but without the part where you pray everything passes.

This helps them understand that privacy is not just an abstract concept, but a tool to protect their wellbeing.

### *5. Final reflection*

"What would you like someone new to know about you… without you having to say it?"

A simple question that opens deep and sometimes surprisingly revealing conversations. Many students realise that what they want to communicate does not match what they actually show, and that is where conscious construction begins.

# 5

# Why it matters (a lot): university, employment and relationships

There is a sentence we hear very often when we talk about the Internet: *"what happens online stays online"*. And, honestly, we wish that were true. The problem is that, in real life, the digital world and everyday life are no longer separate. They mix all the time. What you post, what you comment on, what you share, what you like and what you ignore all become part of your story, even when you think you were just "killing time".

This chapter exists because, although it can sound exaggerated, **digital identity already affects three key areas of life**: academic future, professional future and relationships. Not because the Internet is the enemy, and not because we should live in fear, but because a large part of our lives now happens in places that keep a record. And that record does not always understand context, inside jokes or "I didn't really mean it like that".

At university level, for example, the digital world can be a huge advantage. Projects, scholarships, initiatives, participation and talent are often discovered and shared online. But it can also become a barrier if what appears about you suggests poor judgement, lack of respect or irresponsibility. This is not about being perfect. It is about understanding that **small decisions can open doors, while others can quietly close them**.

The same thing happens with work. Companies do not only look at your CV; they look for signals. How you communicate, the kind of digital footprint you leave, whether you seem able to work with others, whether you look responsible or whether you appear to create problems. Sometimes this feels unfair. But it happens. And the sooner you understand it, the sooner you can use it in a positive way: not to pretend to be someone else, but to show a clear and responsible version of who you really are.

Then there are relationships, which are often the most sensitive area of all. Digital spaces do not only amplify the good things, such as connection, support and community. They also amplify the difficult ones: misunderstandings, impulsive reactions, comparisons, jealousy, exposure, screenshots and messages sent without thinking. A relationship can grow through trust, or it can be damaged in minutes by a post that seemed "harmless".

This chapter is not about frightening anyone or asking for a perfect digital life. It is about something much more useful: **understanding that your online presence has real consequences**, and that with a bit of awareness, it can work in your favour. Because even if you cannot control everything the world thinks about you, you can increasingly control how you present yourself, how you look after yourself and how you treat others.

And in the long run, that makes much more difference than it may seem.

## 1. Digital reputation has real-world impact

In the past, reputation was built in small circles: school, the neighbourhood, the extended family. Today, reputation has a global audience. Anyone can form an opinion about you without ever meeting you in person.

This directly affects three essential areas (like I mentioned in the introduction of this chapter):

### *A) University and further study*

Many higher education institutions will look at an applicant's digital presence when they have several candidates who appear very similar. They are not hunting for mistakes. They are looking for signs of maturity, interests, habits and responsibility.

### *B) Employment*

More and more companies do an "informal search" of a candidate's name. It is not spying. It is simply trying to understand who you are beyond the CV.

In practice, they usually type your name into Google or search on social media to get a first impression: how you communicate, what interests you show, what projects you have shared and whether there is any content that might raise questions. They are not trying to catch you out. They are checking whether someone seems to match the organisation's values, whether they come across as responsible and whether their digital presence matches what they say in the interview.

### *C) Social relationships*

Teenagers often meet online first and in person later. A digital image can help friendships… or complicate them.

A profile picture, a recent comment or a thread of posts can create a first impression before you have even spoken face to face. In the same way, a natural, well-kept profile can open doors to healthy relationships, while an impulsive or aggressive profile can push potential friends away.

It also affects social dynamics: what people share, how they interact, the tone they use and the values they communicate online can create connection, or trigger misunderstandings, jealousy or tension that later spills into real life.

## 2. What do universities and employers actually look for?

They look for consistency, maturity and good judgement.

### *1. Genuine projects or real interests*

Creative posts, participation in activities, portfolios, music, sport, volunteering. Things that show that behind the profile there is a real person with real interests and, crucially, some consistency. Universities and employers love seeing signs that a teenager has passions that do not disappear after three days.

You do not need to be a genius. A small project, a drawing, a homemade podcast or even a simple explanation of how you solved a problem in class can make a very good impression.

*2. Striking inconsistencies*

Saying you are responsible, but behaving in the opposite way online. For example: telling an interviewer you love teamwork... and then posting ten stories in a row complaining that "everyone is useless except me".

These inconsistencies are not usually malicious. They are often just the result of typical teenage impulsiveness. Still, they create doubts for whoever is reviewing the profile. It is a bit like promising you are very organised and letting your bedroom speak for itself... except your bedroom is Mordor.

*3. Risk signals*

Aggressive, discriminatory or dangerous content. This includes anything that suggests a lack of empathy, responsibility or awareness of consequences: mocking comments, insults, "jokes" that do not really feel like jokes, risky challenges or joining toxic arguments.

This is not about being perfect. It is about avoiding the internet presenting an exaggerated version of your worst five minutes.

*4. Basic professionalism*

They are not looking for perfection, just general responsibility. No one expects a teenager to have a LinkedIn-worthy profile or a neutral background photo while staring thoughtfully at the horizon. But they do expect basic common sense: not insulting people, not overexposing yourself for no reason, not sharing sensitive personal details and being able to keep some consistency between what you say and what you do.

In short, they want to see that the person, with their strengths and flaws, can behave sensibly without needing a step-by-step instruction manual.

## 3. Clear examples

*Positive example 1: The "project" student*

A teenager uploads a YouTube video explaining how they built a homemade robot. Years later, when applying for an engineering course, that video appears as the top search result.

*Positive example 2: The creative student*

A girl uses Instagram to share her illustrations. Without realising it, she builds a portfolio that she later attaches to her university application.

*Problematic example 1: The "funny" comment*

"University is overrated." The university she applies to finds it. They do not reject her for it, but it does not exactly help.

*Problematic example 2: The video with no context*

A teenager appears in a party video. They are not doing anything wrong, but the editing gives a different impression.

## 4. How to build a digital presence that helps your future

### *1. Teach that the internet is a window*

You do not need to show everything, only what adds value. The internet is like a house with the curtains open: you decide how much people can see from outside.

If you show only what helps, your digital presence becomes more consistent and safer. If you show absolutely everything… well, then it is like living in a reality TV episode without having signed the contract.

Help teenagers understand that every post sends a message, even if they did not mean it that way. If they share only the highlights, their identity looks like a film. If they share only the worst moments, it becomes a soap opera. The goal is balance.

### *2. Encourage positive public projects*

Portfolios, music, drawings, sport, volunteering. Small windows that show the best of them. And they do not need to be epic "save the world in one weekend" projects.

Something authentic is enough: a drawing, a video explaining an experiment, a small digital project, a song, a simple animation, a mini blog.

Think of it like those film scenes where the main character discovers an unexpected talent. When a teenager shares something creative or constructive, they are showing a positive part of their story. And for their future, that can carry more weight than a thousand selfies.

### *3. Clean up old content*

Not because it is "bad", but because it no longer represents the teenager. Just like nobody still wears the clothes they had when they were eight (hopefully), it makes little sense to keep posts from an entirely different stage of life.

Reviewing your digital past is like tidying your room after years: you always find something that makes you think, "Why on earth did I upload that?" And that is fine. Delete it, archive it or set it to private. Cleaning is not hiding. It is updating.

### *4. Build a basic "personal brand"*

This means showing some consistency in interests, style and tone. You do not need to invent a perfect Marvel character (nobody needs Teenage Tony Stark), just show, in a simple way, who you are and what you like.

You do know who Tony Stark is, right? If not… congratulations, you now have homework: start watching Marvel films. Hint: red and yellow suit (and yes, metallic).

A personal brand simply means your digital self makes sense. If you love sport, there should be signs of it. If you love music, it should show. If you are reflective, your posts should reflect that.

It is not about making life complicated. It is about avoiding an identity that looks like it was written by five different scriptwriters.

### *5. Avoid impulsive content*

Breathe before you post. The button is not going anywhere. Most of the posts we regret were created in "Hulk mode": lots of emotion, very little reflection.

Teaching teenagers to wait one minute can prevent enormous problems. If something makes you angry, upset or far too emotional, write it in a private note first. Social media does not punish calm. If anything, it benefits from it. And thankfully, we are not action heroes making choices in the middle of an explosion.

## 5. Practical advice for families

### *Support without controlling*

Asking "How do you feel about your online presence?" works better than "Show me your phone". The first opens a conversation. The second activates defences worthy of a dragon guarding treasure.

Supporting means staying close without invading, showing interest without looking like you have a magnifying glass in your hand.

A realistic example: a teenager receives a negative comment online. If the family reaction is "Give me your phone right now!", they shut down instantly. But if the reaction is "Do you want to talk about what happened?", the conversation opens and tension drops. Sometimes offering a calm space is enough for them to analyse it themselves.

## Talk about the future without dramatising

Saying "This will ruin your life" does not help. Saying "Do you think this shows the best of you?" encourages reflection without turning into a dramatic speech.

Talking about the future should sound like support, not a doomsday prophecy.

A practical example: if your child wants to upload a photo that reveals a bit too much, you do not need a full family trial. A simple question works: "Would you feel as comfortable if someone saw this in five years?" That question, simple and direct, often works better than any lecture.

## Review profiles together

Like checking clothes that no longer fit. We all have posts that, with perspective, make us think, "Oh… maybe that wasn't my finest moment." Reviewing them together helps decide what stays, what gets archived and what gets deleted.

A useful and slightly funny idea: plan a "digital clean-up day". Like tidying the bedroom, but without discovering socks that have been missing since prehistoric times. The goal is that the profile shows who the teenager is now, not who they were years ago.

## Reinforce the positive

Recognise talent and effort. Not everything online is risk. There are opportunities too. If your child shares a drawing, a project, a video or an achievement, treat it as important. That builds confidence and strengthens their digital identity.

A quick (and very real) example: if they upload a photo from a match and you comment "Well done, champion!", that adds something positive. If you comment "You'd better pass maths as well!", that subtracts... and stays recorded for digital eternity. Better to be a cheerleader than a party-pooper.

## 6. Practical advice for teenagers

- **You do not have to impress anyone**. Not strangers online, not classmates, not the algorithm. Your digital identity is not a popularity contest, even if social media sometimes pretends it is.
- **Do not post when you are angry**. Most impulsive posts end in regret. Write what you feel... but in a private note. Wait. Read it again. If it still feels like a good idea, go ahead. If not, congratulations: you have just saved yourself a mess.
- **Do not record without permission**. Even if it seems obvious, recording or posting videos of others can create big problems (and not the "I forgot my homework" kind). Privacy is a right, not an optional filter.
- **Reputation is built through consistency**. You do not need to be perfect. You just need to be coherent. A kind interaction, a good comment or a great project matters more than you think.
- **If something feels wrong, ask for help**. No one is born

knowing how to handle the digital world. If something worries you, confuses you or bothers you, talking will always be better than carrying it alone. The internet has no "undo" button, but conversations can repair a lot.

## 7. Final mini-checklist

- Does your profile help your future opportunities?
- Do you have old posts that no longer represent you?
- Do you understand that your digital reputation matters?
- Could you explain your identity without embarrassment?
- Have you shown any positive project?
- Do you have a balance between fun and responsibility on your social media?

## 8. Suggestions for teachers

### *1. Activity: "Your future digital self"*

Invite students to imagine how a future interviewer, tutor or work placement coordinator might see them online. Then compare that ideal with their current profile.

### *2. Digital reputation workshop*

Analyse fictional profiles and debate what they communicate: safety, creativity, carelessness, responsibility. Use varied examples and let students justify their opinions.

### *3. Before-and-after dynamic*

Ask students to take an invented impulsive post and rewrite it from a more mature perspective. It shows how a small change can completely shift the overall impression.

### *4. Simulation: "Find your ideal candidate"*

Students act as recruiters and evaluate fictional profiles created by the teacher. Then they explain why they would accept or reject each candidate.

### *5. Final project*

Create a simple digital portfolio showing positive interests: drawings, projects, school activities, music, personal experiences or future goals. It should be short, authentic and representative.

## Chapter conclusion

In short, digital identity is like a backpack we all carry. Sometimes it feels heavy, sometimes it pushes us forward, but it is always with us. The important thing is choosing what we put inside.

If we fill that backpack with impulsive posts, unhelpful comments or photos we barely remember uploading, the journey becomes harder. If, instead, we add projects, creativity, responsibility and common sense, the backpack becomes an ally.

And if you still wonder why all of this matters, think about this:

**Your future self is probably already thanking you… and your past self is trying not to spoil too much.**

Because in the end, the internet does not forget, but we can learn to do things better each day.

# 6

# Basic Digital Safety: How to avoid unnecessary scares (and the occasional family drama)

The phrase "digital safety" tends to trigger three extreme reactions:

1. **Teenagers:** "Ugh. Another lecture. I know how the internet works, thanks."
2. **Families:** "My child's phone is a ticking time bomb and there are only 14 seconds left!"
3. **Teachers:** "Can I teach this lesson without someone joining the Wi-Fi with the password '12345'? No. No, I cannot."

The truth sits somewhere in the middle. The internet is not a minefield... but it is not a padded soft-play centre either. It is a place where wonderful, useful, dangerous and absurd things happen, often all at once.

The good news is that digital safety is not about fear. It is about habits and judgement. This chapter is a clear, practical (and humorous) guide to surviving online without losing your mind.

## 1. Real digital threats (and others that sound like a joke but really are not)

Most online scares come from very simple things:

- weak passwords,
- carelessness,
- fake messages that look real,
- accepting requests from strangers,
- oversharing,
- trusting too easily,
- or pressing "Send" before pressing "Think".

Let's take them one by one, calmly… with the occasional laugh along the way.

### *1.1. Passwords: the most repeated tragedy in digital history*

If we made a documentary, it would be called:

**"Terrible Passwords: a story of love and pain"**

And the main character would be the universally dangerous combo: **DogName123**.

*Classic mistakes*

- Using the same password for everything.
- Birth dates.
- School names.
- "I've got nothing to hide."

*Micro-story*

**The day "Sofi2008" got hacked**

Sofía used the same password for TikTok, Gmail, Spotify, the Wi-Fi and probably the Christmas tree lights too. One day she gets: "Your password has appeared in a data breach." She thinks: "But I'm not famous, what would they want from me?" Within an hour, someone had already tried to get into four accounts.

Spoiler: she survived. But now she uses a password manager because her mum almost organised a full family intervention.

*Practical solutions*

- **Use long phrases that are hard to guess.**
- Better than a single word is a whole phrase that makes sense to you but not to others. For example: **MyNeighbour'sCatDoesNotPayForNetflix2024**.
- The longer the password, the harder it is to crack. Three or four words strung together are usually far safer than "Pepito123".
- Avoid obvious details: names, birth dates, your school name, your favourite football team… If someone knows you even slightly, they will try them.
- A good test: if someone who knows you could guess it on a boring afternoon, it is not a good password.
- **Turn on two-step verification.**
- Also called two-factor authentication or "a second barrier".
- It works like this: even if someone guesses your password, they also need an extra code sent to your phone, an authenticator app or your email.

- It is like having a key plus an extra lock: even if you lose the key, the door does not open on its own.
- It is especially important for:
- email,
- main social media accounts,
- gaming accounts with purchases,
- and any service where you have personal or banking data.
- It can feel like an extra step at the beginning, but it is the kind of step that can save you a lot of headaches (and a lot of tense family conversations).

*Quick basic checks to see if you are on the right track*

Even though it is annoying (yes, it is), there are a few express checks we should all do from time to time. Think of them like brushing your teeth: they are quick, but if you do not do them... the problems arrive later.

- **Update your system and apps.** No one gets excited about "an update is available", but updates close security holes. Ignoring them is like leaving a window open when you go on holiday.
- **Check which devices have access to your accounts.** Google, Apple, Instagram, Spotify... most services show you all connected devices. If you see one you do not recognise, like a "Samsung Galaxy" from Uzbekistan, that is NOT normal.
- **Check app permissions.** Some apps ask for more permissions than a teenager trying to come home at 3 a.m. Camera, microphone, location... review them. Many apps do not need that much.

- **Check which social media sessions are still open.** Sometimes we leave sessions open on someone else's computer, a school tablet or even the TV. That is basically inviting the whole internet into your account.
- **Clean up old posts.** You do not need to delete everything, but ask yourself: "Does this still represent me?" If the answer is no, archiving is your best friend.
- **Use a password manager.** It remembers passwords, suggests strong ones and warns you if one has been leaked. It is like having a digital butler who does not judge your choices.
- **Check your backups.** Especially on phones. Having a backup is like having a lifebuoy: you do not appreciate it until the day your phone falls into the toilet.

These mini-checks take about 3–4 minutes each, but together they build a decent digital wall. You do not need to be a hacker or an expert, just willing to spend a little time avoiding big scares.

### *1.2. Impersonation: more common than you think*

It sounds like a film, but the teenage version is less glamorous:

"Someone made an account with my photo and is talking to my friends."

Or worse:

"My cousin messaged me… but it wasn't my cousin."

### *Why it happens*

Because copying a photo and a name is easy, and we tend to trust what we recognise. On social media we react fast: we see a familiar face, a known name or a normal-looking message and assume it is legitimate. That split second of automatic trust is exactly what impersonators take advantage of.

Sometimes they even write like us, copying our expressions or emojis, which makes it feel even more convincing. And to make things worse, many platforms display real and fake accounts in almost identical formats.

### *Simple (but very effective) tips to spot impersonation quickly*

You do not need a master's degree. You just need to pause for three seconds and check these clues:

- **Look at the username.** If your friend is called María López and the new account is **M4ria.Lopez__Official**, something smells off. Your friends do not usually become "premium versions" of themselves.
- **Check the profile picture.** Is it the same photo, but cropped or pixelated? Too perfect? Like a stock photo? Bad sign.
- **Notice how they write.** We all have a style. If your cousin never uses emojis and suddenly texts: "Hiiii ", it probably is not your cousin... or they have been possessed.
- **Verify outside the app.** Call them, send a voice note or message them on another platform. If your friend says, "What new account?", mystery solved.
- **Be suspicious if they ask for something.** Photos,

codes, money, personal information… real friends do not suddenly message you for your ID "just because".

- **Check the account creation date.** Many platforms show it. If the account was created two hours ago, this is not exactly a long, trustworthy relationship.

These tips seem obvious, but in daily life we get caught busy: cooking, studying, doing homework support. Pausing for a moment prevents a huge number of problems.

### *1.3. Phishing: the art of tricking you without you realising*

Phishing is the Picasso of digital scams: it looks authentic… until you examine the details. And like abstract art, everyone claims they understand it, but many do not.

At first glance the message looks legitimate, polite, professional… but when you look closely you find suspicious brushstrokes: spelling mistakes, random urgency and links that look like they were typed by a haunted keyboard.

#### *What is phishing, exactly?*

It is a scam designed to make you reveal personal information, passwords, banking data, codes or even your peace of mind, by making you believe you are speaking to someone trustworthy.

It is like a stranger wearing your favourite hoodie, copying your way of speaking and walking into your house saying, "It's me, open up."

*Why does it work so well?*

Because it plays with three universal human weaknesses:

- **Haste.** No one thinks clearly when they see a message like: "URGENT, YOUR ACCOUNT WILL BE CLOSED IN 24 MINUTES!"
- **Curiosity.** A parcel? A prize? An unexpected refund? Our brain is already celebrating before checking anything.
- **Fear.** "Your account has been blocked", "we detected unusual activity", "you must update your details"... nothing makes a finger click faster than a small scare.

*A "visual" example (no museum paintings involved)*

Imagine you get a message from your bank. Everything looks normal... except:

- the logo looks like it was made in Paint 2002,
- the sender is "real-bank-security-trust-me@hotmail.com",
- the link begins with "http://definitely-not-a-scam-trust-me.ru".

And still people fall for it because they are cooking dinner, helping with homework or watching a series and respond without thinking. That is exactly what scammers want.

*Real examples*

- "Your parcel could not be delivered, pay 2.99€ here." (You did not order anything.)
- "Your bank has blocked your account, enter this link." (Your bank does not talk like that.)
- "Hi, it's Mum, I lost my phone, send me money." (Mum is in the living room watching a series.)

*Micro-story*

**The time Lucas's dad almost bought a castle in Moldova**

He receives: "You have won an international property prize." He thinks: "I never entered, but hey, you never know."

Luckily, Lucas says: "Dad, if it were real, they wouldn't email you from 'winnermoldavia2024@bricosexpress.com'."

*How to avoid it*

This is where we move from panic to strategy. Avoiding phishing does not require a cybersecurity degree. It requires pausing, checking details and applying a few simple rules. Here is a clear and expanded version, with (of course) a touch of humour.

1. **Distrust alarmist messages**

The aim of phishing is to make you anxious so you stop thinking. If a message sounds like:

- "Final warning!"

- "Your account will be deleted NOW!"
- "Hurry or you will lose access forever!"

understand that 99% of the time it is pressure tactics. Real companies do not write emails like the final boss of a videogame.

Quick tip: if it speeds up your heartbeat, slow down. Breathe. Read it again.

1. **Do not click suspicious links (even if curiosity bites)**

Links are phishing's favourite weapon. They look normal but lead to fake copies of official websites.

Before clicking:

- hover over the link (or press and hold on mobile) to see the full address,
- if you see weird words, strange domains or a missing letter ("gogle.com", "banc0seguro.net"), it is a trap,
- golden rule: never open a link sent by message if you were not expecting anything.

Realistic example: if the postal service texts you about a parcel and you have not ordered so much as an eraser... be suspicious.

**What if you actually ARE expecting a parcel or an alert?**

This is phishing's master trick: sometimes it matches real life. You really are expecting something, and your guard drops.

So even if the timing feels perfect, do not trust it just because it "fits your life right now".

Safe method:

- Go to the official website by typing the address yourself

(no links),

- Or open the official app (amazon, your postal service, your bank),
- Check there whether there is actually a notice, issue or message.

If the app is normal but the message screamed "URGENT, YOUR PARCEL IS HELD", you know what it was: a well-timed trap.

Think of it like this: if someone knocks on the door on the exact day you expect a delivery, you still do not open without checking the peephole, right? Online, the peephole is the official app or website.

1. **Always check the sender**

Sometimes the name looks trustworthy, like "SuperSafeBank", but the address is:

ban.co.security@online-alerts-pro.net

Real companies use professional domains, not emails that look like they were created in a café with free Wi-Fi.

Key signs it is fake:

- long domains that make no sense,
- lots of numbers and hyphens,
- spelling mistakes,
- addresses that do not match the real institution.

1. **Turn on two-step verification (your extra shield, yes, mentioned earlier, yes, I know, I'm stubborn)**

Even if someone falls for the trick and hands over a password, two-step verification blocks access. So even if you mess up, you still have a lifebuoy.

Especially important for:

- email (the key to all your accounts),
- social media,
- online banking,
- gaming platforms.

Bonus: if you receive a verification code you did not request, someone is trying to get in.

1. **Verify the information through another channel**

If you receive a message "from the bank", do not reply to the message.

Do this instead:

- Go to the official website by typing it yourself,
- Call the number on your bank card,
- Ask directly.

If it was fake, they will clarify immediately.

1. **Learn the typical phishing signs**

About 90% of phishing attempts share these:

- Exaggerated urgency,
- Requests for personal data,

- Threats or dramatic warnings,
- Prizes that are too good to be true,
- A strange or incorrect tone,
- Suspicious links.

If a message has two or more, treat it like it is on fire.

1. **Most importantly: assume nobody is giving you free things**

Phishing survives on "just in case". But no, you have not won a house, an iPhone, a trip or a ham without entering anything.

1. **AI and phishing: the paradigm shift**

Until now, phishing had "giveaway signs": spelling mistakes, badly cropped logos, suspiciously dramatic messages. Artificial intelligence is changing the rules, and that forces all of us, teenagers, families and teachers, to be more alert than ever.

What has changed?

Before, many fake messages were obvious because they looked rushed or poorly written. Today, thanks to AI:

- Messages are much better written,
- The tone imitates real companies,
- Grammar and spelling often look perfect,
- They can even mimic how a specific person writes.

This means the "it sounds weird" detector is no longer as reliable as it used to be.

AI that writes like your bank (or your cousin)

AI tools can generate emails, texts and messages that sound 100% professional. They can copy:

- the formal style of a bank,
- the carefully polite voice of a delivery company,
- or the typical phrases of someone you know.

Not because AI "knows you", but because scammers can give very detailed instructions:

"Write a polite, convincing and urgent message like a bank asking for data verification."

And AI does it... better than many humans.

Why is this a real problem?

Because our psychological barrier drops. Before, we were protected by the thought:

"This is written so badly it must be fake."

Now the messages have:

- Perfect tone,
- Professional structure,
- Logos placed correctly,
- Clear instructions.

Conclusion: it is increasingly difficult to tell real from fraudulent.

What can we do? Change our mindset.

AI makes phishing smarter, so we must become more cautious. No more impulsive clicks.

New rules of the game:

- Distrust first, verify after, even if the message looks

flawless,

- Do not trust "professional tone" (now everyone can sound professional),
- Always use the official website or app, more than ever this is the safe refuge (yes, i know, i said it already, but i am still stubborn, you know me),
- Assume anyone can imitate anyone, well-written does not mean legitimate,
- Enable official notifications and filters, real companies use clear, verifiable channels.

A simple example

Before:

"Your pakage iz stoped, pay hier 2,99€" equals fake in 0.2 seconds.

Now:

"Dear customer: We have detected an issue with the delivery associated with your address. To release the parcel, please review the pending information via the following verified link."

It is scary how convincing it can sound… and how quickly we could fall for it if we do not pause.

Final message: AI improves phishing, but it can also strengthen your defences

The good news is that the same AI scammers use can also protect us: browsers, email apps and security systems use advanced algorithms to detect fraud.

But nothing replaces this:

a three-second pause before clicking.

That tiny habit is worth gold.

### *1.5. Oversharing: posting too much without thinking*

You do not need to share your whole life to have an online presence. But certain posts can reveal far more than you realise, even when they seem completely harmless.

*Risky examples (and why they are risky) 1*

1. **Photos with location enabled**

Sometimes the risk is not what you see in the photo, but what you do not see: metadata. A single image can include the exact street where it was taken, the time and, in some cases, GPS location.

This can allow strangers to:

- identify where you live or study,
- know when you are usually home or out,
- rebuild your daily movements.

Example: you upload a photo in your bedroom. No problem... except the automatic tag says "Street X, 19:32". Now a stranger knows your location with surgical precision.

1. **Visible school uniforms**

A uniform does not only show where you study. It can reveal your city, the areas you move around and what time you arrive and leave.

Combined with other posts, it becomes a pretty accurate

map of your routine.

Example: uniform photo + “on my way to school” post + posting time equals location and schedule confirmed without meaning to.

1. **Timetables, addresses and routines**

Constantly posting:

- “I leave school at 17:00”,
- “Training every Tuesday at 18:30”,
- “We’re always at that park”,

creates a pattern anyone can follow.

This is not about living in paranoia. It is about understanding that repeated information makes it easier to predict where you will be and when.

1. **Posts showing entrances, keys or the inside of your home**

Sometimes the danger is not the photo itself, but what sneaks into the background:

- The lock brand,
- An open window,
- An identifiable object,
- The house layout,
- Or even keys on a recognisable keyring.

These are not obvious details... until someone looking for

information analyses them.

1. **Announcing the house is empty**

The classic summer post:

"We're going away for two weeks, goodbye world!"

It sounds innocent, but it is basically a digital neon sign saying: "THERE IS NOBODY HOME, COME IN AND HAVE A LOOK."

Even if your profile is private, there is always a risk of screenshots, forwarding or accounts you did not fully control.

*In summary*

Oversharing is not dangerous because of one isolated detail. It is dangerous because each detail is a puzzle piece. Put several pieces together:

- location,
- schedule,
- uniform,
- routines,

and you get a complete picture.

The key is not to stop posting. The key is to post with common sense.

Funny example:

"I'm going on holiday for two weeks, here's my house, here are my keys, take care."

### *1.6. Emotional safety: when digital life affects you inside*

There are not only technical risks, but emotional ones too. Screens do not bite, but what happens behind them sometimes does.

#### *Why does it matter so much?*

Because for teenagers, digital life is not separate from real life. It is part of it. What happens online directly affects mood, self-esteem and relationships.

#### *Common situations that hurt*

- **Negative comments or mockery:** a simple "that's cringe" can hit harder than adults realise.
- **Constant comparison:** perfect bodies, perfect lives, perfect success… even if half of it is fake. A teenage brain does not always separate performance from reality.
- **Pressure to be constantly available:** if you do not reply fast, "you're angry"; if you do not post, "you disappear". Exhausting.
- **The feeling of not belonging:** if you are not in the group photos, if nobody tags you, if nobody mentions you, it can feel like real exclusion.

*What do teenagers need?*

- safe spaces to talk without fear of judgement,
- constant reminders that digital life is edited,
- families who support without minimising ("it's nothing") and without catastrophising ("this is horrific").

*Reflection*

The internet does not need to be perfect, just safe.

### *1.7. Video games and chats*

Online games are wonderful... until they are not. For many teenagers, this is their main social space. But like any social space, it comes with risks.

*Typical risks (in plain language)*

- **Chats with strangers:** anyone can pretend to be a teenager. Sometimes they are, sometimes they are not.
- **Insults or harassment:** anonymity is the best friend of the "digital tough guy".
- **Requests for personal data:** age, city, photos... chats have no real control.
- **Requests for photos or videos:** this should never become normal.
- **Pressure to move to private social networks:** "Give me your Instagram so we can talk later." Not always a good sign.

*How to support without banning*

- talk about not sharing personal information,
- teach how to block and report,
- agree on time limits and spaces for gaming,
- show interest: "Who are you playing with? What are you doing?"

*Golden rule*

"If you wouldn't talk to that person in real life, don't do it in the chat."

## *1.8. Ephemeral apps*

Apps that promise "everything disappears" are the digital equivalent of writing a message in the sand: poetic, yes, but someone can take a photo before the wave arrives.

Here is the problem: many teenagers think "ephemeral" means "safe", when in reality it is only ephemeral in theory.

Let's break it down properly, step by step.

*Why are they risky? (expanded explanation)*

These apps create a false sense of privacy because:

- Screenshots exist (even if the app warns you, the receiver still has it),
- Forwarding exists (in milliseconds it can move from one person to a group of 30),
- Screen recording exists (and the app does not always detect

it),
- External cameras exist (yes, one phone filming another phone; technically tragic, but effective),
- Many platforms keep content longer than they claim for moderation, safety or legal reasons,
- Nothing guarantees the receiver is who they say they are,
- You may think you are sending something to a trusted person… and that may not be true.

*What risks can this create?*

This is where things become more serious. Ephemeral apps can lead to:

- Unwanted sharing of photos or videos, including intimate content,
- Emotional pressure or blackmail, especially in teenage relationships,
- Social conflict when a "private" image becomes public,
- Damage to digital reputation, because a screenshot lasts forever,
- Guilt or shame, even when the mistake was not fully yours.

*What teenagers need to understand (in more detail)*

- "It disappears" does not mean "there is no trace". It means you can't see it anymore… but someone else might still have it.
- Intimate content can never be 100% controlled. Once sent, it is out of your hands.
- If something can be used to hurt you, someone might

try, not always out of pure cruelty, sometimes out of immaturity, impulsiveness or stupidity.
- Impulses last seconds; screenshots last years.

*Clear examples so they actually get it*

- "It was only for my partner." Then their best mate has it too because "I showed him to get his opinion."
- "It was just a silly video, it disappeared in 10 seconds." Captured in 0.3.
- "It's fine, I trust this person." Great… until you don't.
- "Everyone does it." Yes, and that is why everyone has at least one story they would rather forget.

*How to explain it without sounding like a lecture*

- It is not "DON'T DO IT", it is: "If you choose to do it, do it with your eyes open and knowing the real risks."
- Practical examples work better than abstract speeches.
- Remind them: making a mistake does not ruin your life. The key is asking for help if something gets out of control.

*An important message*

Nothing disappears completely. If you don't want it to circulate, don't send it.

### *1.9. What to do when there is a REAL hack*

When a hack happens, the brain goes into panic mode. The heart races, your finger trembles, and the universal phrase appears: "They've stolen everything!"

Calm down. A hack is serious, yes, but it is not the end of your digital world. The key is acting quickly and in order, not in "chaos mode".

Here is a clear, expanded guide designed to reduce drama.

#### *Signs you have been hacked (if you are still not sure)*

- You cannot log in, even though the password is correct.
- You receive verification codes you did not request.
- You see posts or messages you did not write.
- You see devices logged in from impossible places (hello, "Samsung South Korea").
- You get warnings about suspicious login attempts.
- Your friends say: "Why did you ask me for money?" while you were peacefully having a snack.

If even one of these happens, treat it as real. Waiting is worse.

#### *Clear steps (explained calmly and properly)*

1. **Change your password immediately**

Think of it as closing the door when you feel a draught. Even if it's already half open, close it.

- Use a completely new password,

- Avoid reusing old ones,
- Avoid names, dates and anything predictable.

1. **Check which devices have access**

Google, Apple, Instagram, TikTok and other services show connected devices.

- if you see something like "iPhone 12 – Canada" and you haven't left town since 2018, remove it,
- log out of all sessions just in case.

1. **Turn on two-step verification (yes, again)**

This is not nagging, it is digital love. Two-step verification turns your account into a house with a double lock.

- even if the attacker has the password, they cannot get in without the extra code,
- especially important for: email, social media, banking, games.

1. **Tell friends and family if your account has been used to impersonate you**

If someone used your account to ask for money, info or photos, people need to know.

- a simple line works: "I've been hacked, ignore any strange messages."
- it is not embarrassing, it happens to loads of people.

1. **Breathe. Then act.**

Panic leads to bad decisions: deleting things without thinking, reinstalling apps, or falling for "recovery services" that are also scams.

- take a breath,
- follow the steps one by one.

1. **Check apps connected to your account**

Sometimes the problem is not the social network, but an external app you gave permissions to years ago.

- remove access for anything you do not recognise,
- treat it like cleaning out a digital storage room.

1. **Contact official support**

Platforms often offer:

- specific hack recovery forms,
- temporary account locks,
- recovery via documents or selfies,
- review of suspicious activity.

If money is involved, contact immediately:

- Your bank,
- Your mobile provider (if your sim was duplicated),
- Or the police, if appropriate.

*Extra tips most people don't mention*

- Change passwords on every account where you used the same one. Yes, it is annoying. Yes, it is necessary.
- Check purchases, subscriptions and automatic payments. Sometimes they test with a small payment first.
- Enable login alerts so you know if someone tries to access your account.
- Check your recovery email. If that is compromised, everything else is too.

*Micro-example (realistic)*

"Claudia noticed she couldn't log into Instagram. She changed the password, good. But she didn't check connected devices, bad. The attacker was still logged in. Moral: closing the door doesn't help if the thief is already in the living room."

*Reassuring message*

A hack is stressful, yes, but you can regain control if you know what to do and stay calm. The key is acting quickly, checking everything patiently and strengthening security so it does not happen again.

## 2. Practical advice for teenagers

Teenagers do not need a technical manual, they need clear rules they understand and remember.

Advice explained:

- You do not have to impress anyone. The algorithm is not your boss. Posting under pressure means posting without thinking.
- Do not post when angry. Today's rage becomes tomorrow's regret. Half of digital problems start with impulses.
- Do not record without permission. Respect is the foundation of any digital coexistence.
- Your reputation is built day by day. Every post adds or subtracts. Everything has impact.
- Ask for help without fear. Nobody is born knowing how to manage the internet. Talking early prevents bigger messes.
- Think before accepting requests. Not everyone is who they claim to be.
- Turn off location services if you don't need them. You do not need to announce where you are to the world.
- Do regular digital clean-ups. If it no longer represents you, archive it.

## 3. Practical advice for families

### *Support without controlling*

Controlling creates silence; supporting creates trust. Teenagers are not intimidated by the internet. They are intimidated by adults who overreact. That is why "Show me your phone" often slams doors shut.

Instead, phrases like these work far better:

- "Do you want us to check it together?"
- "If something makes you uncomfortable, tell me without fear, I'm not going to shout."

- "Do you want me to help you set it up so it's safer?"

They communicate support, not surveillance. The goal is not to inspect, it is to be available.

*Talk without exaggerating*

No threats like "The internet will ruin your life!" and no careless messages like "It's fine, it's only a photo." The best approach is proportionality.

Teenagers shut down when adults overreact, but they also shut down when their issues are dismissed.

A balanced approach sounds like:

- "This isn't the end of the world, but it is important."
- "Let's understand what happened and how to avoid it next time."
- "You're not being punished: you're learning."

The goal is guidance, not drama.

*Review profiles together*

Reviewing a profile is not an interrogation, it is a kind of "digital fitting". Just as you choose clothes that match who you are, you choose which posts reflect your identity.

You can make it natural:

- "Shall we look at your profile together and see if it represents you the way you want?"
- "Do you want help organising your posts or improving

privacy?"

This opens conversations about privacy, old photos, unknown followers and what their identity looks like from the outside.

*Reinforce the positive*

If you only point out mistakes, teenagers stop telling you things. If you also celebrate what they do well, they open up.

Instead of focusing only on impulsive posts, notice:

- When they create something original,
- When they debate respectfully,
- When they help others online,
- When they use the internet to learn, organise or express themselves.

This strengthens their digital self-esteem, which matters as much as real-world self-esteem.

And remember: every time you validate a good digital choice, you increase the chance they will repeat it.

## 4. Practical advice for teachers

*Activity 1: "Scam detectives"*

The teacher presents real and fake examples of messages, emails or posts. In small groups, students analyse:

- what signs raise suspicion,
- what parts seem legitimate and why,

- what questions they should ask before trusting.

Each group shares conclusions. The aim is not to get it right every time, but to practise explaining why something feels trustworthy or not.

*Activity 2: "Before and after"*

Students receive a set of impulsive, exaggerated or risky posts (location enabled, personal details, aggressive tone). Their task is to transform them into safer, more respectful and more responsible versions.

This works well as a paired mini workshop: in pairs they review examples, explain what they would change and why, then share the best versions with the class.

*Activity 3: "The ideal candidate"*

The teacher gives three fictional profiles (they can be invented characters, famous animals or humorous references). Each profile includes posts, comments, photos and digital choices.

Students evaluate:

- who has the best digital reputation,
- who inspires the most trust,
- who might face problems in the future,
- what changes they would make to improve each case.

Perfect for discussing consequences without preaching.

### *Activity 4: Positive portfolio*

Each student creates a mini digital portfolio showing:

- real interests,
- skills,
- school projects,
- creative activities,
- personal achievements.

The aim is to understand that a digital footprint can help you too. It is not only about avoiding risk, it is also about building presence consciously.

It can be a poster, a presentation, a simple page or even a shared document. The key is reflecting on what image it communicates.

## 5. Short micro-stories

### *Story 1: The eternal password*

Hugo used "password123" since 2017. One day it stopped working. It wasn't magic, it was a leak. Now he uses a manager… and a dictionary.

### *Story 2: The phishing message that almost fooled the dog*

The family gets a "bank" SMS at 03:17. The dog barks. The dog was right.

*Story 3: The gamer and the friendly stranger*

He accepted "PabloXD92" thinking it was his cousin. Spoiler: it wasn't his cousin. It was an adult trying to get personal information.

## 6. Chapter conclusion

Digital safety is not about paranoia, it is about power. It is understanding that every click, every photo, every comment and every password contributes to something bigger: your digital identity, that version of you that lives online and, like plants, grows depending on how you care for it.

Because in the end, what we have seen in this chapter can be summarised very simply:

- You protect your accounts, you strengthen your identity.
- You think before you post, you shape your reputation.
- You spot scams, you avoid dramas that leave a footprint.
- You support your children or students, you help them build a sensible digital self.

The internet is not a monster, but it is not a teddy bear either. It is like a bicycle: wonderful when you know how to ride it, dangerous if you go downhill with no brakes. And your digital footprint is the path you leave behind. It can be a tidy trail, a well-lit motorway… or a labyrinth worthy of a horror videogame. The difference is your decisions.

Think about this: if digital identity were a sticker album, which stickers would you want repeated? Which ones would you rather nobody had? That mental image helps more than you'd think.

And as always, a few basic rules to finish:

The best security tool is your brain, plus a bit of humour and a pinch of common sense.

- If you're not sure, don't post.
- If it makes you uncomfortable, talk.
- If something sounds too good to be true… it is.
- And if your digital footprint could speak, it should say: "This person knows what they're doing."

# 7

# Building a Positive Digital Presence

Up to this point in the book, we have learned how not to put our foot in it online, how to understand the trail we leave behind, and how to recognise that algorithms are a bit like that cousin who "just wants to help" but somehow manages to complicate your life without meaning to.

Now it is time for the nice part: not only avoiding problems, but actually building something good.

Creating a positive digital presence is not about being perfect. It is about using the internet as a window that shows the best of you, without letting everyone see the chaos behind the curtain, much like we all do when surprise visitors turn up.

## What it Means to Have a Good Online Reputation

Online reputation is like a digital perfume: sometimes pleasant, sometimes overpowering, sometimes unforgettable… for better or worse.

It is what others think of you based on:

• your posts, which you may say "mean nothing" but actually say quite a lot;

• what you comment, because even a simple "haha" can be

interpreted in ten different ways depending on who reads it;

• how you respond, especially when someone disagrees with you and your tone reveals more about your character than any photo ever could;

• what you share, from interesting links to memes that might make your teacher raise an eyebrow;

• and what others share about you, because the internet has a wonderful ability to preserve photos and videos that you would never have chosen as your official public image.

Having a good online reputation does NOT mean:

- Looking perfect, as if you lived inside a digital magazine every day;
- Having thousands of followers, because popularity is not the same as good judgement;
- Pretending your life is flawless, when we all know that off screen your bedroom is still a battlefield.

It DOES mean:

- Being respectful even when others are not, showing that you do not need to set fire to a comment thread to defend your point;
- Thinking before you post, a bit like pressing the mental button that says "am i sure i want this to exist forever?";
- Showing real interests, because authenticity is always more appealing than a collection of digital poses;
- Keeping coherence between what you say and what you do, a quality that is increasingly rare in a world where it is easy to preach calm while arguing furiously in a group

chat.

*Example*

Two profiles:

**Person A**

They comment respectfully, share projects, and help from time to time. They are the kind of person who does not need to seek attention to be liked. Their profile is consistent: a school project, a personal achievement, perhaps a photo with friends without dramatic filters. When they comment, they do so politely, even when they disagree. If they make a mistake, they apologise without turning it into a drama. They do not get involved in endless arguments, do not respond to provocation and, above all, do not post soap-opera-style indirect messages. Their digital presence communicates calm, responsibility and that reassuring feeling that, if you worked or studied with them, you would not need to check their history to see what bomb might go off tomorrow. In short, Person A is the digital equivalent of someone who arrives on time, brings their own pen and even shares their notes.

**Person B**

Spectacular photos, constant arguments, endless indirect messages. Their profile looks more like a Netflix trailer than a personal account. Everything is intense: perfect photos, deep quotes, motivational reels, selfies that suggest they are always about to publish a book. But among all that visual perfection, the details appear: arguments in the comments, indirect messages so obvious they could come with names attached, cryptic stories that generate more drama than information, and passive-aggressive replies that make spectators reach for popcorn. Person B is not necessarily a bad person; they simply live online as if every day were the final of a reality show. The result is a digital reputation that may look shiny at first glance, but leaves a feeling of instability. Teachers, employers and even friends are never quite sure what to expect. It is the kind of profile that makes you think: "Amazing photo... but what happened ten minutes before this?"

Who inspires more trust in a teacher or a future employer? Spoiler: Person A. Not because they are the "good one" in the example, but because they transmit stability, judgement and a kind of digital coherence that is worth its weight in gold today. When a responsible adult looks at online profiles, they are not searching for perfection or epic sunset photos. They are looking for signs of maturity, responsibility and someone who is unlikely to turn the staff room or office into the next season of a reality show. Person A represents exactly that. Calm, reasonable and reassuring. Person B may be visually fascinating, but leaves doubt. And in a world saturated with digital impulsivity, calm is a superpower.

## Portfolios, Creativity and Healthy Projects

A digital portfolio is the modern version of "look what I can do", without forcing your parents to invite half the family over to admire a drawing or school project. It is the natural evolution of the cardboard folder, except now it fits into a link and does not take up space in the living room.

It can be hosted on:

- A simple website, even if you are just starting out;
- A google site, practical, clean and proudly "i made this

myself";
- A themed instagram account, ideal for those with a clear hobby and the desire to show it, especially useful for current or future artists;
- A blog, perfect for people who have things to say without being interrupted;
- Or a well-organised folder, which is already more than can be said for most digital desktops on the planet.

*Why is it so powerful?*

1. **It shows real skill, not appearances.**

A portfolio does not need filters, poses or late-night philosophical quotes. It shows what you can actually do, not what you pretend to do.

1. **It builds self-esteem based on ability.**

Not on likes, views or "your dog is cute", but on real achievements, even small ones, that grow over time.

1. **It opens real doors.**

Competitions, scholarships and opportunities often appear where you least expect them. A small, well-made portfolio can catch the attention of the right person.

1. **It helps you discover what you are good at.**

Sometimes teenagers do not know they have a talent until they upload a few similar projects and realise they genuinely enjoy it.

### *What to include*

A portfolio is a creative buffet. The more variety, the better.

- Art: drawings, designs, photos, from quick sketches to pieces that could survive a strict art teacher's critique;
- Science: experiments, summaries, visual explanations that show you understood the topic, or at least tried;
- Technology: websites, robots, coding projects, even those that did not work perfectly, because learning counts;
- Humanities: essays, reflections, podcasts, anything that shows you can think, analyse and express ideas without emojis;
- Sport, music, hobbies, everything fits as long as it shows a genuine part of who you are.

### *Perfection is not the goal*

Not everything needs to look like a Pixar production. No one expects perfect lighting or studio-quality sound. A portfolio is an album under construction. Some pages shine more than others, some repeat themselves, and some might be slightly bent. Together, they tell a story. And a well-told story can open more doors than a thousand perfect selfies.

## How to Create an Authentic Digital Identity

Being authentic online does not mean sharing everything. It is not a public confession exercise or an open diary. It means that what you share is not theatre. That you are not performing for an invisible audience, trying to appear more interesting, deeper, happier or more perfect than you really are. Authenticity means showing a realistic version of yourself. A cared-for version, yes, but a recognisable one. Not turning every post into an award-worthy digital performance. The internet does not need another series protagonist. It needs people who resemble real people.

### *1. Coherence*

You do not need a marketing plan, but you do need a bit of continuity. Your online presence does not have to be rigid, but it should not feel like it is written by a rotating team of scriptwriters. If one week you appear to be a philosophy expert, the next a personal trainer, and the next a food critic, even the algorithm will stare at the screen wondering which version is scheduled today. Coherence is not repetition. It is being recognisable without changing character every five minutes.

Think of it like clothing. You can experiment and evolve, but if one day you wear a suit, the next an astronaut costume and the next a pirate outfit with no context, people will not know whether to greet you, ask for an autograph or call a professional.

*2. Express your real voice*

You do not need to sound like an influencer reciting motivational quotes from a minimalist penthouse while holding a suspiciously cold coffee. Nor do you need to write as if every sentence were destined for a Pinterest wall. Your real voice is the one you use with friends, teachers and family, yes, even when you are slightly more polite than usual.

When someone reads you and thinks, "Yes, this person really could speak like this in real life", you are doing it right. It is incredibly freeing not to imitate others or adopt an exaggerated tone to appear deeper or smarter. The internet is full of people trying to sound like fictional characters. Those who simply sound human are refreshing.

*3. Do not exaggerate to fit in*

The internet detects exaggeration as quickly as a teenager notices you used the wrong emoji. It never fails. Everyone shares special moments, but when every breakfast looks like a luxury resort, every reflection sounds like a book opening and every photo has studio lighting, suspicion appears. If you do not eat avocado toast surrounded by scented candles and highlighted books, you do not need to pretend you do. If your life is not a mix of mindfulness, sunrise yoga and extreme productivity, congratulations. You are human. Pretending is exhausting and unsustainable. Authenticity is far more attractive than any filter.

### *4. Emotions, yes, but with balance*

Sharing emotions is healthy. Sharing all your emotions in real time, publicly and at two in the morning is another matter. Emotional overexposure turns your profile into a public roller coaster. Entertaining for observers, exhausting for the rider. Balance does not mean being cold. It means not turning your social media into a permanent loudspeaker for emotional ups and downs.

### *5. Share processes, not only results*

We love seeing progress because it reminds us that people grow and learn. Showing real processes, including mistakes and drafts, builds authenticity. Watching someone move from "I have no idea what I am doing" to "look what I achieved" teaches more than only showing the final product. It also inspires others. Learning is not linear, and showing the path removes pressure and builds connection.

## From Consumer to Creator: a Smart Path

Consuming content is easy. Creating it is powerful and surprisingly addictive in a good way. When you create, your brain switches from autopilot to laboratory mode. You think, test, fail, adjust and discover that intentional thinking feels good.

### *Reason 1: creativity organises the mind*

Creating is not just about "having a brilliant idea and that's it". Creating forces you to slow down a little, much more than when you are choosing between two recommended videos. When you build something, a text, a drawing, a video, a school project, you have to organise your thoughts, decide what comes first, what comes next, what is unnecessary and what deserves a central place. It is like tidying a chaotic drawer: not glamorous at all, but it leaves your mind much clearer than any productivity filter ever could.

Creativity also helps the brain switch off "digital autopilot mode" and start working more like a laboratory: you try, you fail, you fix it, you try again… and suddenly you discover that thinking with intention is actually quite enjoyable. Who knew?

### *Reason 2: it forces you to reflect*

A consumer moves from video to video like someone opening the fridge without knowing what they want. A creator, on the other hand, starts asking deeper questions, such as:

- "Why do I want to do this?"
- "What do I want to communicate?"
- "Does this really make sense… or am I just carried away by my enthusiasm at 11:48 pm?"

That reflection turns creation into a kind of mirror: it shows you thoughts you did not even realise you had. There is no need to become philosophical; it is enough to recognise that, when you create, you listen to yourself a little more.

### *Reason 3: you learn practical skills*

Creating digital content is the secret gym for 21st-century skills. While you are trying to stop a video from being crooked or making a paragraph sound less chaotic, without even noticing it you are learning to:

- Edit
- Design
- Write better
- Communicate clearly
- Solve problems
- And, occasionally, stay calm when your file mysteriously disappears

These skills are useful far beyond the Internet. They help you at school, in personal projects and, one day, in real jobs where nobody will ask you to make a TikTok, but they *will* expect you to explain things clearly.

### *Reason 4: it protects you from impulsiveness*

When you are only a consumer, you react quickly: you see something, you feel something, you comment, you post... and only later you think, "Maybe that was not the best moment to say that."

But when you are working on a creative project, your relationship with the Internet changes. Your posts stop being impulses and become decisions. When you are building something that matters to you, you are more careful about what you upload, how you say it and the impact it may have.

It is as if your own work acts as a gentle but effective brake against digital outbursts.

### *A metaphor*

Watching *MasterChef* is fun, inspiring and perfect for commenting from the sofa. But trying to make the soufflé yourself... well, that is when you really learn about technique, patience and the mysterious laws of gravity. The digital world works in the same way: watching is pleasant, but creating is what transforms you.

And yes, sometimes your soufflé will collapse. But other times, it will turn out so well that you will want to show it to the world.

## A guide for families

### *1. Help your children find "their thing"*

Everyone has a talent... even if it is sometimes hidden like lost lunch boxes at school. And no, that talent does not have to turn them into professional streamers or follower collectors. "Their thing" might be drawing, writing, playing an instrument, cooking, photography, programming, building things, solving problems or telling stories.

Your role as an adult is not to push them towards a specific skill, but to support them while they discover what makes them shine, even if that light takes time to turn on or flickers like an old bulb.

When they find something they care about, the Internet stops being just consumption and starts becoming creation. And that is where the magic begins.

### *2. Celebrate creation, not perfection*

What matters is trying. The learning process is full of drafts, improved versions and things that do not work the first time (or the tenth). If you only celebrate perfect results, your child will learn to hide mistakes like classified secrets.

If, instead, you celebrate effort, curiosity and motivation, the Internet becomes a place to grow, not a shop window where everything must sparkle.

Imperfect creation builds creativity. Absolute perfection builds anxiety. We choose the first one.

### *3. Talk about reputation as you would talk about the future*

Online reputation is like planting a tree: what you do today will give shade tomorrow... or it will not. There is no need to scare them as if every post were a final exam, but it *is* important to remind them that every photo, comment or project becomes part of their digital story, a story others may see before meeting them in person.

A calm conversation works much better than a dramatic speech.

"What you upload builds your story. Let's make sure it tells something you like" opens doors rather than closing them.

### *4. Help them organise their portfolio*

Digital chaos *can* be organised, even if it sometimes feels like an archaeological expedition through folders called "STUFF2", "final_final_NOW", or "DO NOT DELETE IMPORTANT".

Organising a portfolio does not mean turning it into a professional exhibition; it means helping them decide what deserves to be shown, what can be kept as a memory and what probably belongs in the drawer of forgotten things.

An organised portfolio does not only look better, it also helps them see their own progress without relying on memory alone.

### *5. Remember what really matters*

Digital identity is part of their wellbeing. It is not just technology: it is self-esteem, safety, expression, relationships and future opportunities. Supporting them does not require knowing more about the Internet than they do (spoiler: that is probably impossible), but showing them that there is an adult who listens, does not laugh at their doubts and understands that growing online is simply part of growing up.

## A guide for teachers

### *1. Encourage creation in the classroom*

You do not need to turn every lesson into an audiovisual workshop worthy of a school film festival, but it *is* essential to open small spaces for students to create. That space can take many forms: a short explanatory video that is not trying to win an Oscar but does show understanding; a simple blog entry where they can write without interruptions; a digital poster that summarises a complex idea better than ten minutes of explanation; a portfolio of progress; or a small project they can proudly show in class.

The key is for students to discover that creating leaves a more valuable trace than simply consuming content. Watching a video is comfortable; making one forces thinking, organisation and responsibility. And yes, students usually take much more care online when they are sharing their own work. Nobody wants their project labelled "disaster of the term".

*Practical classroom examples*

1. **30-second explanatory video**

Topic: the water cycle, a maths operation, a spelling rule.

Goal: explaining something aloud using their own words. Recording themselves shows them they must truly understand the content.

1. **Digital poster on a difficult concept**

Reducing an idea to one image often requires deeper understanding than writing two pages. Colours, icons and structure force clarity, even if someone uses far too many colours at first.

1. **One-entry blog**

A short reflection: what they learned, what surprised them, what connects to real life. Not about writing like a novelist, but about thinking.

1. **Term portfolio**

At the end of the term, students choose their best work, explain why and reflect on what they would improve. Honest progress matters more than polish.

1. **Collaborative mini project**

For example, creating a tutorial for another class. Students learn content, teamwork and digital responsibility, skills they will use all their lives.

Creating spaces for students to create turns the classroom into more than a place to receive information: it becomes a laboratory where everyone has something to contribute.

*2. Talk about reputation without lectures*

A lecture about digital reputation lasts in a teenager's mind for less time than a 24-hour story. A well-chosen real case, calmly explained, can stay with them for years. Use anonymised examples from social media and ask: what happened, why did it happen and what could have been done differently, without apocalyptic warnings.

*Practical examples*

- A misunderstood comment
- A viral challenge that went wrong
- A "perfect" profile with hidden warning signs
- A screenshot that broke trust
- A thoughtless "like" and its message

These activities help students understand digital reputation as a series of small decisions with real impact.

### *3. Integrate digital identity exercises*

Simple but powerful activities: analysing fictional profiles, comparing intention and perception, and discussing how small digital gestures build identity. Students are often surprised to see how differently others interpret the same post.

### *4. Teach how to build a portfolio*

A portfolio does not need to be perfect. It needs to be *theirs*. It should show process, learning, mistakes and progress. Teachers do not need professional editing skills, just time, listening and encouragement.

Ideas like "before and after" work brilliantly, as does the "mistake of the month" section. Turning errors into learning reduces anxiety and normalises creativity.

### *5. Remind them that they can improve*

Digital identity is not fixed. It is editable. Remind students that they can change, correct and grow. The idea that "what I post defines me forever" creates anxiety; the idea that "I can improve" builds responsibility without fear.

Exercises like "version 2.0", rewriting an old post, show growth clearly and positively.

## Conclusion

Building a positive digital presence is not a one-day project or a mission for tech heroes. It is a continuous process of small decisions and moments of reflection. This chapter is not about becoming influencers or giving up fun. It is about combining creativity with responsibility and authenticity with common sense.

Mistakes will happen. Filters will be questionable. Some posts will age badly. That is part of growing up, online and offline.

A positive digital presence is not inherited or improvised. It is built.

And now, you know how to start.

## Conversations That Matter: How to Talk About All This Without the Drama

Talking about digital identity, online reputation, privacy, risks, positive creation and all those modern concepts can feel, at first, like trying to explain why your phone decides to update at the worst possible moment. In other words: frustrating, slow, and with a small risk of ending up saying, "Never mind, we'll look at it another day."

By this point in the book, many of the topics we'll cover here have already appeared. And it's not because we're repeating content like this is a resit exam, but because some conversations are so important they need to be looked at from different angles.

A bit like when a teenager says, "I'm fine," and you know there's actually a whole chapter behind it.

This chapter exists because understanding the digital world is one thing... but talking about it without turning it into a drama is something else entirely. And we need it. A lot. Because you can have all the theory from the book: know what a digital footprint is, recognise the risks, understand online reputation... but if you don't know how to talk about it at home or in class, it all stays as a nice PowerPoint in your head.

Here we'll look at:

- How to have family chats without it sounding like a three-hour lecture;
- How to listen without invading, that slightly magical skill that mixes patience, tact, and avoiding questions that feel like a police interview;
- What to do when a digital problem appears, because it will at some point, and that's normal;
- And also what *not* to do, because there are typical mistakes that make everything harder (and we want to avoid them).

And yes, we'll do all this with humour. Not the "joke every two lines" kind, but enough to remind you that talking about these things doesn't have to be a soap-opera-level drama.

Breathe. These are important conversations, yes... but they can also be really nice conversations.

Spoiler: it's easy to say, but doing it isn't always easy. Still, we have to try (this is for parents and educators), teenagers, please, can you make it just a little bit easier for us?

## Family Chats Without Lectures

Talking to teenagers about their digital life can feel like trying to change a lightbulb on a very high ceiling: you know it needs doing, you don't want to break anything, and you know you could lose your balance at any moment. But don't worry: here we're going to make these conversations more human.

First, it helps to understand that a chat is not a lecture. If you start with "We need to talk," your child will probably switch to mental aeroplane mode. Instead, something like "I saw something interesting about social media and I wanted your opinion" opens doors rather than closing them.

*Tricks for conversations that don't feel like a chore*

1. **Ask open questions.** Instead of: "Why did you post that?" (CSI voice), try: "What did you like about that post?" It changes the whole vibe.
2. **Share before you ask.** If you share a small story of your own (a mistake, a scare, something you learned), the mood softens. Suddenly you're not speaking "as a parent", but "as a human who also gets things wrong".
3. **Use humour as a way in.** "I saw a video that made me think of you… don't worry, it wasn't an embarrassing dance." People usually appreciate the effort.
4. **Talk in neutral moments.** While cooking, walking, or in the car. Avoid intense face-to-face moments; they can feel like a job interview.
5. **Don't jump to conclusions too fast.** If you don't have all the information, don't fill the gaps by imagining the entire season of a teenage drama. Let them tell their version first.

## How to Listen Without Invading

Listening to a teenager without looking like a spy satellite is a skill worthy of international recognition. But it can be done. And not just done, done well: calmly, with tact, and with a small dose of humour so the conversation doesn't feel like a press conference after a disaster. Listening without invading is a subtle art: strategic patience and knowing when to step back.

### *What does "listening" really mean?*

It's not nodding while your brain is making a shopping list or checking whether you turned the oven off. Listening is being present, properly. It's showing that their experience matters, that you're not there to judge, and that your job in that moment isn't to fix the world, but to understand it through their eyes.

It also means resisting the temptation to translate every sentence into "What have you done now?" or to jump ahead like you already know how the episode ends. Sometimes listening is simply letting the story come out, even if it starts in total chaos or needs three attempts before it makes sense.

A teenager notices immediately if you're listening or if you're on autopilot. They also notice if you're just waiting to deliver a life-lesson. That's why listening without invading needs three key things: time, real interest, and self-control.

### *Practical rules*

1. **Don't interrupt to correct every detail.** Even if you think they're exaggerating or retelling it their way. First you listen; then you help. Accuracy can wait, trust can't. And yes, this isn't always easy. Many adults (me included) find it really hard not to jump in with "Wait, that's not exactly what happened." But holding back is part of the skill.
2. **Validate without approving.** "I understand that made

you angry" doesn't mean "You were right to insult someone." It means: "Your feelings make sense, and now we'll look at how to handle it without setting half the class on fire." Validating is recognising emotion, not justifying behaviour.

A typical example: "I get why that reply in the group chat annoyed you; anyone would be bothered." That gives you space to follow with: "But insulting half the group wasn't the best move, was it?" This takes practice. A lot of practice.

1. **Ask before giving advice.** "Do you want ideas, or do you just want me to listen?" This sentence is pure gold. It saves unwanted speeches, reduces defensiveness, and stops every chat turning into an unrequested life tutorial. Adults love giving advice, it comes out automatically, but not everyone wants solutions in the middle of frustration.

And sometimes the answer will be a clear "No, I just want to talk." Then you accept it. No drama. No forcing advice through the back door. Sometimes you just breathe and think: "Right, today I listen, tomorrow we'll see."

1. **Avoid 'interest' that sounds like spying.** Asking "And who was online?" too insistently usually raises more suspicion than answers. Interest yes; military interrogation no. If you seem desperate for details, the other person will shut down as tightly as a brand-new iPhone's privacy settings.

Teenagers spot disguised surveillance instantly. If they sense a hidden radar, trust disappears. And when trust goes, they stop talking.

1. **Respect silence.** Sometimes they take time. Sometimes they don't know how to start. Sometimes they're choosing how to explain the embarrassing bit without dying of shame. Silence isn't failure; it's part of the process.

Think of it like a computer "loading": if you interrupt too soon, the app crashes. Give space. And yes, sometimes the silence feels long. But often that's when they finally speak, and they speak better because they didn't feel rushed.

## What to Do When a Problem Appears

Breathe. Properly. Before you speak, before you think about consequences, before you imagine worst-case scenarios worthy of a thriller series, breathe. Every young person has a digital slip-up at some point. Adults do too, even if some of us keep them filed away in the mental folder called "better not revisit." The difference isn't whether a problem appears, but how we react when it does.

A digital problem is not the end of the world. It's a sign. A sign that something happened, that someone needs help, and that there's a real chance to learn. And yes, it can be hard to see it like that when your heart races and your protective instincts switch on like an over-sensitive alarm.

### *Step 1: stay calm*

The energy you bring is the energy they absorb. If you panic, they panic. If you stay calm, there's space for a real conversation.

Being calm doesn't mean you don't care. It means you choose not to react in the heat of the moment. You can feel angry, worried or scared, but you don't need those emotions to drive the conversation. A calm adult sends a strong message: "This matters, but we can talk about it."

### *Step 2: gather the facts*

No extras, no assumptions, no Hollywood plot with dramatic soundtrack.

"Tell me exactly what happened, take your time."

Simple and direct. It opens more doors than asking ten questions in a row. Get the full story before you decide what it means. And yes, it might come out messy. That's normal.

### *Step 3: avoid "I told you so"*

It's a very human instinct... and also completely unhelpful. "I told you so" fixes nothing, teaches nothing, and usually just creates shame or anger.

You might be right. You might have seen it coming. But saying it in that moment doesn't help. The goal isn't to win an imaginary argument, it's to support someone dealing with a real problem.

### *Step 4: look for solutions with them, not for them*

This is where learning happens. Instead of imposing a solution from above, sit down and think together.

- **Do we need to delete something?** Not deleting just to delete, but thinking about whether that content still adds anything or whether it's now causing more trouble than it's worth. Sometimes deleting is smart; other times learning to manage it is better.
- **Do we need to tell a trusted adult, a tutor, or a teacher?** This often causes resistance, but it's important to normalise that asking for help isn't "snitching", it's getting support when things are too big to handle alone.
- **Is it better to block someone or report behaviour?** Blocking can give immediate peace. Reporting can stop the same thing happening to others. Talking through both options teaches thoughtful decisions, not impulsive ones.
- **Can we change settings to stop it happening again?** Privacy, comments, tags, visibility, reviewing these isn't punishment, it's learning. It turns a mistake into a real improvement.

Guide them, but let them be involved in fixing it. When they take part, they gain control, responsibility and confidence. It's not "mum or dad fixes everything," it's "we deal with problems with support."

### *Step 5: turn it into learning*

No drama, no mocking, no minimising. Just linking the situation to what can improve next time.

"Okay, it was messy… but what would you do differently next time?"

That question changes everything. It looks forward, not backwards. It helps close the episode without leaving it as an open wound.

### *Step 6: end with support*

This is key, and often forgotten. After talking, analysing and planning, make one thing clear:

"I'm with you."

"You're not on your own."

"This doesn't define you."

The final message should be support, not threats or hidden warnings. The point is: "I'm here. You don't have to fix this alone." That's what makes the difference between hiding the next mistake… or feeling safe enough to talk.

## What to Do When a Problem Appears (for you, teenager or not-so-teenager)

Right. Something happened online and it wasn't nice. Maybe someone said something that hurt, maybe you shared something and it didn't go how you expected, maybe you felt attacked, confused, or just overwhelmed. First of all: breathe. You're not the first person this has happened to and you won't be the last. And most importantly, this does not define you.

The first helpful move is to stop. Don't reply in the heat of the moment, don't send the message you *really* want to send, don't post a story full of indirect digs that will only make things worse. Anger has terrible aim when it comes to digital decisions.

### *Step 1: don't deal with it alone*

Your first instinct might be: "I'll handle it," "It's not that big," or "If I tell someone, it'll turn into a massive thing." That's normal. Almost automatic. Nobody enjoys explaining a digital mess, feeling watched, or thinking they'll disappoint someone.

But trying to carry it alone usually makes it heavier and last longer. Talking to someone you trust, an adult, a teacher, a family member, isn't snitching or overreacting, even if it feels like it from the inside. It's asking for help when something is too much, the same way you would if you had a physical pain or didn't understand a subject at school.

Also, when you're inside the problem, everything looks bigger and more hopeless than it really is. An outside view often brings calm, ideas and solutions you can't see from inside. And no, that doesn't mean they fix everything for you, it means you don't have to carry it alone.

### *Step 2: say what happened, without adding extras*

No need to exaggerate or downplay it. Tell it as it was. Say what happened, who was involved, how you felt, and what you're most worried about now. You don't need perfect words or all the answers, just honesty.

If you struggle, it's fine to say: "I don't really know how to explain it" or "It feels weird saying this." That matters too. Sharing feelings helps the other person understand why it's weighing on you.

Hiding parts of the story out of fear usually makes the problem grow in silence. Telling it calmly, even if it feels a bit embarrassing, often brings more relief than you expect. And yes, saying it clearly and honestly is already a huge first step, sometimes the hardest one.

### *Step 3: think in options, not punishments*

When a digital problem appears, there are usually a few ways out. And no, none of them automatically start with "My life is over" or "I reply right now and burn everything down."

Options might include:

- Deleting content that no longer helps or is causing conflict,
- Blocking or muting someone to get your peace back,
- Reporting behaviour if it's clearly crossed a line,
- Adjusting privacy settings to reduce future exposure,
- Asking a trusted adult, teacher or mediator for help.

Not every option fits every situation, and that's fine. The important part is remembering you have choices, and choosing on purpose gives you something you really need: a sense of control. Moving from "something horrible happened" to "okay, I can do a few things" changes how the problem feels.

Options also stop impulsive reactions. Impulse usually leads to fast, messy decisions (and messages you later wish you could erase from the history of the internet). Options help you act with your head.

### *Step 4: learn something from it*

This isn't about finding someone to blame or analysing your mistake like it's an international crime. It's about learning. Ask simple but powerful questions: What would I do differently next time? What signs did I miss? What have I learned about myself, other people, or how the internet works?

When a mistake becomes learning, it stops being just a bad moment and becomes experience. Experience isn't always fun, but it's very useful.

### *Step 5: remember the main thing*

One online problem doesn't erase all the good in you or everything you've done well so far. Your digital identity isn't just one mistake, one bad day, or one impulsive decision. It's built over time, through lots of small choices, adjustments, corrections and growth.

In the middle of a problem, it can feel like everything is falling apart. But it isn't. A stumble doesn't define who you are or who you can become. It's part of learning how to move in a complicated digital world.

And yes, this is something you learn too.

## What Not to Do (Common Mistakes That Make Everything Worse)

Now we're in universal territory. These mistakes happen in homes everywhere.

### *Mistake 1: reacting like the world is ending*

A classic. And extremely effective… at ruining any conversation. When a digital problem appears and the immediate reaction is full "red alert", shouting, blaming, threats, dramatic speeches like an apocalyptic film trailer, the result is predictable: communication breaks.

For parents, it often comes from fear: fear that something will go wrong, fear you missed it, fear you've lost control of a situation you don't fully understand. That's understandable. But when fear turns into an emotional explosion, the message the teenager hears isn't "I care about you," it's "This is dangerous and it's not safe to tell you." Next time, they won't.

For teenagers, it feels like a small mistake has suddenly become an irreversible disaster. Even if there's a solution, what they feel is judgement, anger, and "I messed up and now everything will get worse." The result is silence, defensiveness, or lying to avoid another explosion.

Turning the volume down emotionally doesn't mean you're ignoring the problem. It means you're creating a space where you can talk without fear. A calm adult shows control and support. A teenager who feels listened to is far more likely to explain what happened honestly.

### *Mistake 2: taking the phone away as the first option*

Confiscating the phone can feel like a quick fix, like turning something off and on again. But in the digital world, removing the device doesn't solve the real problem. It just covers it up… badly.

For families, it sends the message that the problem is the

phone itself, when usually the issue is use, situation, or lack of guidance. It also turns the chat into immediate punishment, which massively reduces the chance they'll talk next time. The lesson becomes: "If I tell them, I lose my phone." So next time, they won't tell you.

For teenagers, it often feels like a huge injustice and not connected to what happened. They don't experience it as help, but as forced disconnection from their social, academic and emotional world. And honestly, they're not always exaggerating: today the phone is diary, notebook, friends, entertainment, and sometimes a refuge.

And let's be realistic: taking the phone away doesn't remove the internet. It just creates teenagers who use other devices you don't control: a friend's phone, an old tablet, a school laptop, the family computer "just for homework"... Connection doesn't disappear; it becomes invisible.

This doesn't mean there should never be limits or consequences. It means the phone shouldn't be the automatic first reaction. It should be the last option, thought through calmly and explained properly.

### *Mistake 3: spying "to protect"*

This mistake usually starts with good intentions: fear. Fear that something will go wrong, fear you won't find out in time, fear the digital world is too big and too fast. The problem is that spying doesn't protect, it creates a temporary illusion of control.

Checking messages, reading chats in secret, accessing accounts without saying so... may feel like caring. But what the teenager receives is: "I don't trust you." And when trust breaks, problems don't disappear, communication does. After that, mistakes aren't prevented; they're hidden better.

For teenagers, discovering their privacy was invaded often feels like betrayal. Even if the adult meant well, the line was crossed. And then the next time, they won't talk, even if they need help, because they fear losing their space.

Extreme surveillance doesn't teach decision-making or responsibility. It just delays problems until they arrive bigger and harder to solve.

This isn't about ignoring everything and hoping it's fine. It's about changing approach: support instead of surveillance, asking instead of spying, clear agreed rules instead of secret actions.

Important point: parental controls are not the enemy. They're useful, especially at the beginning. But they work best when agreed, explained and talked about, not imposed silently. And they shouldn't last forever. As maturity and trust grow, controls should reduce, like taking the stabilisers off a bike. The goal isn't to monitor forever, but to support until it's no longer needed.

### *Mistake 4: minimising their worries*

"That's nothing." "You're worrying about silly things." "You'll get over it." These often come out without bad intention, but the effect is clear: the other person shuts down.

What teenagers feel matters, even if it looks exaggerated from the outside. Minimising doesn't make the worry disappear; it just pushes it into a corner where it stops being shared.

Adults often do this because of perspective: you've seen worse, you know the world doesn't end because of a comment.

But a teenage brain doesn't run on perspective; it runs on emotional intensity. What looks "small" to you can feel like the centre of the universe for them for a few hours or days.

Recognising emotion doesn't mean making it bigger. It can be as simple as: "I can see this has affected you." Then you can put it in context later. Without emotional validation, there is no real conversation.

### *Mistake 5: turning the chat into a police report*

When a chat becomes a chain of questions ("Who was there? What did they say? What time? Why? What did you do next?"), it stops being a conversation and becomes an interrogation. And nobody talks naturally when they feel questioned.

Adults often think lots of questions show interest and control. Teenagers often experience it as pressure, distrust, or a trap. Result: short answers, avoidance, or silence.

A good conversation doesn't need every detail from minute one. It needs space. A few key questions, not a full questionnaire. If they start answering in one-word replies or looking at their phone like it's an emergency exit, pause, breathe, and bring the tone back to human.

Teenagers can help here too: if the conversation feels overwhelming, say it calmly. "I feel a bit stressed with so many questions," or "I'd rather explain it little by little," or "I don't know how to say it properly yet." That isn't disrespect, it's setting a healthy boundary.

### *Mistake 6: analysing everything from your adult perspective*

"Well, when I was your age..." is classic, and almost always unhelpful. Not because adult experience is worthless, but because the context has changed massively. Digital life adds exposure, speed and permanence that many adults didn't have at that age.

Adults often compare to calm things down. Teenagers hear: "You don't get it." And in some ways, they're right: it's not the same.

This doesn't mean adult experience is useless. It means you need to understand today's context first. Replace "When I was your age..." with "Tell me how you're experiencing this." It changes everything.

And a message for teenagers: when an adult says "When I was your age...", they're usually not trying to compete with you. Often they don't know how to help, so they grab the only tool they have: their own experience. It can sound annoying, disconnected, or pointless, but it usually comes from worry and a genuine desire to protect you. Adults are learning as they go too, sometimes.

### *Mistake 7: using sarcasm at the worst moment*

Sarcasm can be funny and quick... but it can also be deeply hurtful at the wrong time. When someone is worried, embarrassed or insecure, a badly timed joke can shut the conversation down instantly.

Adults sometimes use sarcasm to reduce tension without going serious. Teenagers often experience it as mockery or disrespect. Humour is brilliant for connection, but only when the other person is ready for it. In the middle of a problem, what helps most isn't a clever line, but being taken seriously.

A simple rule: if the joke would make you laugh in that situation, fine. If not, save it.

*How a teenager can respond without attacking*

If you hear "When I was your age..." and you switch off inside, that's normal. But you can help stop the conversation crashing. You don't have to respond with anger or sarcasm. Sometimes you just need words for what you need.

Possible calm replies:

- "I get what you mean, but right now it would help more if you just listened a bit."
- "I know you're trying to help, it's just that my situation feels different."
- "Your experience matters, but first I need to explain how it feels for me."
- "I'm not looking for comparisons right now, I'm trying to work out what I can do."

These don't attack, don't reject the adult's intention, and make something clear: you want support, but you also want to be understood in your context. That's not rude, that's mature communication.

And if it still isn't working, it's okay to ask for a pause: "Can we talk later when we're both calmer?" Sometimes the best move is not pushing forward, but giving both sides time to breathe.

## Material for Families and Teachers

This section isn't here to give magic formulas or universal solutions (if only). It's here to offer simple, realistic ideas you can use day to day. Because good communication isn't about being a psychology expert or reading every book in the world, it's practice, intention, and patience. A lot of patience, sometimes.

### *Practical ideas for families*

- **Set up chat moments without screens.** No need for a formal "family meeting". Simple everyday moments work: cooking, walking the dog, being in the car. Times when the phone isn't the main character and talking feels easier.
- **Create "safe spaces" for conversation.** Moments where they can talk without fear of instant punishment. It doesn't mean no consequences ever, it means you listen first, understand, then decide. When a teenager knows everything won't instantly turn into a telling-off, they speak more.
- **Go through basic phone settings together.** Doing it together feels like support, not control. And it's also a chance for adults to learn (and yes, sometimes the kids explain how things work).
- **Talk about your own digital mistakes.** Sharing your own slip-ups normalises learning and lowers perfection pressure. It shows mistakes are part of the process and admitting them is okay.
- **Accept that it won't always go smoothly.** Some chats will be awkward, some silences uncomfortable, and some-

times you'll think "this isn't working." That's normal. Communication isn't a straight line; it's more like a road with bends and a few bumps.

*Practical ideas for teachers*

- **Classroom activities to practise digital communication.** Small, relaxed tasks that explore common situations reduce drama and encourage reflection without pointing at anyone. You don't need complex sessions or to be a social media expert, just use situations students recognise (a chat misunderstanding, a misplaced comment, a screenshot shared without permission) and talk them through calmly.
- **Fictional cases to discuss real problems.** Invented examples let you discuss digital conflicts without exposing anyone's real life. Students engage more when they don't feel judged. You can even exaggerate slightly (with a bit of humour) so risks and consequences are clearer.
- **Role-play family conversations.** Acting out different viewpoints builds empathy in a way theory rarely does. One student plays the teenager, another the worried adult, another observes. Then discuss how each role felt, the conversations can be surprisingly honest.
- **Digital empathy activities.** Questions like "How would you feel if this happened to you?" or "What would you think if you saw this with no context?" help students understand real impact online. It teaches a key point: online we don't see tone, gestures, or facial expressions, so messages can hurt more than the sender expects.
- **Remember teachers don't have to know everything.** Supporting students isn't about having every answer. It's

about creating space for dialogue and reflection. Saying "I don't know, let's think it through together" can be one of the best things you do. You don't need to be an expert in every app; you need to be an adult who is available, consistent, and willing to listen.

### *Practical ideas for teenagers*

(yes, you, the one reading this who spends more hours online than you'd admit out loud)

Before we start: nobody expects you to do everything perfectly. Not your parents, not your teachers, not even you (even if it sometimes feels like it). Digital life isn't a final exam. It's ongoing trial, error and learning. These ideas aren't here to control you, but to help you move through a world that, honestly, goes too fast sometimes.

1. Learn to pause before posting (even if it is hard)

Not everything that comes into your head needs to become a post. Really.

Before uploading something, ask yourself three quick questions:

- Would I still post this in a week?
- Would I mind if someone I do not know very well saw it?
- Am I posting this because I want to… or because I need attention right now?

If you are unsure, stop. It is fine not to post it. The Internet will not end if you do not publish anything today. Believe it or not, it will survive.

Pausing is not censoring yourself, it is giving yourself time.

And time usually improves decisions quite a lot.

1. Do not reply in the heat of the moment (the Internet hates impulsive replies)

When something annoys you, upsets you or hurts you, your brain switches to "reply NOW" mode. The problem is that this mode usually has very poor judgement.

Replying while angry often leads to:

- Messages you later want to delete.
- Arguments that grow bigger and bigger.
- Screenshots that last forever.
- And delayed regret.

Practical advice:

Write the message,

Do not send it,

Wait a bit,

Read it again.

Very often, after a few minutes, you think: "Right... maybe not".

1. Learn to use the "block" button without feeling guilty

- Blocking is not weakness.
- Blocking is not overreacting.
- Blocking is not losing an imaginary battle.

Blocking is setting a boundary.

And setting boundaries is a very adult skill, even if it sounds strange.

If someone makes you feel bad, provokes you constantly or does not respect your limits, you do not have to put up with it to prove anything. You do not have to convince anyone. You do not have to explain yourself again and again.

Your peace of mind is worth more than an endless comment argument.

1. Remember that not everyone shows the full truth

Most profiles show:

- The best angle,
- The best moment,
- The best version,
- And zero visible problems.

Comparing your real life with the edited version of others is unfair… to you.

It does not mean you are doing something wrong. It means you are only seeing one piece of the puzzle.

If you ever feel that "everyone is doing better than me", remember this: you are not seeing anyone's full day, only their shop window.

1. Talking to an adult does not take away your independence

This is important:

- Asking for help does not mean you cannot cope alone,
- It means you know when something is too much for you.

Talking to a trusted adult is not giving up or "making things worse". Sometimes it is exactly the opposite: stopping a problem from growing.

And yes, the adult may react oddly at first. They may worry too much. They may say something unhelpful. They do not always get it right (spoiler: nobody does).

But most adults do not want to control your life. They want to help… even if they do not always know how.

1. Learn to say "this is not helping me" without being rude

If a comment from an adult annoys you or does not help, you can say so, and you can say it well.

Examples that work better than getting angry:

• "I understand what you are trying to say, but right now it would help me more if you just listened."

• "I know you are worried, I just need to explain it in my own way."

• "At the moment I do not need solutions, I just need to talk."

This is not answering back.

It is communicating better.

1. Look after what you post… but also how you use the Internet

Your digital identity is not only what you upload.

It is also:

- Which accounts you follow,
- What content you consume,
- How much time you spend online,

- How you feel after using a social network.

If an app leaves you feeling worse than before, something is wrong.

It is not always your fault, but you can make small changes: mute accounts, unfollow, reduce time, change habits.

It does not have to be all or nothing. Sometimes small adjustments are enough.

1. You do not have to be a perfect creator or a digital activist

You do not have to:

- Have an opinion on everything,
- Take a position all the time,
- Reply to every controversy,
- Prove that you know more than everyone else.

You can use the Internet to create, learn and express yourself without living in constant debate mode.

Your digital identity also includes knowing when not to say anything. And that, even if it does not look like it, is a form of maturity.

1. If you make a mistake (because you will), learn and move on

You will mess up at some point. For sure.

Everyone does.

The key is not avoiding all mistakes (impossible), but:

- Recognising them,
- Learning something,
- Adjusting,
- And moving forward.

An online mistake does not define you.

How you react afterwards does.

1. Remember this (really important)

You are not alone in the digital world.

You do not have to know everything.

You do not have to do everything perfectly.

Your digital identity is built little by little, through small decisions, adjustments, uncomfortable conversations and constant learning.

And asking for help, setting boundaries, thinking before posting and looking after how you feel online does not make you less free.

It makes you more in control of your digital life.

In short, talking matters, and how we talk matters even more. Digital conversations do not need perfection, they need consistency. It is not about getting it right every time, but about keeping on trying, even when it is difficult. Because listening without invading, speaking without judging and supporting without controlling is a shared learning process, both inside and outside the classroom.

In the end, talking matters, and *how* we talk matters even more. Digital conversations don't need perfection; they need consistency. It's not about getting it right every time, but about keeping trying, even when it's hard. Because listening without invading, speaking without judging, and supporting without controlling is a shared learning process, both inside and outside the classroom.

In the end, talking matters, and *how* we talk matters even more. Digital conversations don't need perfection; they need consistency. It's not about getting it right every time, but about keeping trying, even when it's hard. Because listening without invading, speaking without judging, and supporting without controlling is a shared learning process, both inside and outside the classroom.

# 8

# Practical Tools for Digital Life

## Real solutions for a real (not ideal) world

So far, we've talked about ideas, attitudes, conversations and shifts in perspective. All very necessary, yes... but let's be honest: that's not the whole story. In reality, we've already been sharing advice, examples and small practical ideas throughout the book (or at least I hope so, otherwise this author doesn't come out looking great).

Still, and here comes the part where I admit I can be a bit repetitive, I've decided to dedicate a whole chapter just to this. Because it never hurts to have everything together, organised, and firmly grounded in real life. And yes, I know: I insist a lot. I'm aware. I accept it. And I'm sorry.

At some point, someone usually puts their hand up (mentally or out loud) and asks:

"Okay, all this sounds great... but what do I actually *do*?"

This chapter exists to answer that question.

Because digital life isn't managed with good intentions alone.

It's managed with tools, settings, habits and small practical decisions that, added together, make a huge difference. We're not aiming for perfection, that doesn't exist, but for something much more realistic: reducing risks, gaining peace of mind, and not losing our sanity along the way.

You won't find magic formulas or endless, impossible checklists here. You'll find what actually works day to day, both at home and in the classroom.

## Basic Privacy Everyone Should Understand

Digital privacy isn't about hiding, living in fear, or putting on an imaginary trench coat every time you open an app. It's about deciding who can see what, when, and why. In other words, having a minimum level of control over your own digital life.

Just as we don't leave the front door open "just in case", or invite strangers to snoop around the living room, it doesn't make much sense to leave our entire digital life permanently on display. Not because we have something to hide, but because not everything is for everyone.

Privacy isn't paranoia. It's common sense. It's deciding that some things are public, some are for friends, and others stay personal. Exactly like real life: you don't say the same things to your best friend, your teacher, or someone you've just met in a queue.

Managing privacy is really about learning to set healthy digital boundaries. Boundaries that don't isolate you, but do protect you. And although checking settings or thinking twice before sharing can feel like effort at first, that small investment of time usually saves a lot of scares, misunderstandings and unnecessary drama later on.

### Key ideas worth keeping in mind

Before diving into settings, buttons and screens full of options, it helps to be clear about a few basic ideas. They're not technical, they don't require expertise, and yet they prevent a huge number of problems. They're like traffic rules for digital life:

simple, repeated endlessly... and surprisingly ignored.

- **Privacy is not secrecy.** It doesn't mean hiding bad things or living in permanent incognito mode. It means protecting what's personal and choosing what you share, with whom, and in what context. Just like offline life.
- **Public content travels further than you think.** Much further. It can reach people you didn't expect, at moments you didn't anticipate, and be interpreted in ways you can't control. What seems harmless today can resurface tomorrow out of context and be far less funny.
- **Default settings are rarely the best ones.** They're designed for the platform's growth and data collection, not for your wellbeing. Adjusting privacy isn't being suspicious, it's being aware.

## Basic (but very important) habits

We're not talking about extreme sacrifices, radical changes, or turning your digital life into a Wi-Fi-free monastery. We're talking about small, simple habits that are perfectly manageable and, when repeated regularly, make a big difference to peace of mind, safety, and avoiding problems that could have been prevented with two clicks and a bit of attention.

These habits aren't about living on constant alert. Quite the opposite: once internalised, they stop taking up mental space. Like looking before crossing the road, they become automatic.

- **Check who can see your posts.** Not just once in a lifetime or only when something goes wrong. Platforms change, you change, and what felt fine before may not feel fine now.

- **Decide who can comment, tag you or message you.** Not everyone needs direct access to you or your digital space. Limiting this isn't rude or antisocial, it reduces noise, misunderstandings and awkward situations.
- **Think twice before sharing real-time location.** Especially when it reveals routines or frequent places. You don't need to hide, just avoid giving more information than necessary. Sharing later is often enough.
- **Assume anything you send can leave the chat.** Not because others are bad people, but because screenshots, forwards or misunderstandings happen. Thinking about this beforehand saves a lot of regret.

These habits don't eliminate all risks, but they reduce the chances of unnecessary trouble enormously. And that's already a big win.

A simple and surprisingly effective rule of thumb:

If you wouldn't feel comfortable seeing it at a family gathering in five years' time, you probably don't need to post it.

## Useful Settings on Phones and Social Media

Phones come set up as if we were calm, organised adults with infinite self-control. Spoiler: we're not. And that's okay. Not teenagers, not many adults, and not even the people who design these apps live with that level of constant restraint.

For teenagers, this means something simple: if you use your phone exactly as it comes out of the box, it's not because you "lack willpower", but because it's designed to keep you inside, not to help you disconnect. Adjusting notifications, usage limits or permissions isn't cheating, it's levelling the playing field a bit.

For families, it means understanding that changing settings isn't overreacting or being distrustful, but offering realistic support. Just as there are rules about sleep, study or going out, reviewing digital settings is part of learning. It's not punishment, it's education.

Tweaking settings isn't an obsession or a warning sign. It's a practical response to an environment designed to grab attention nonstop. Adjusting your phone doesn't reduce freedom, it gives some control back.

*Settings worth reviewing*

- **Notifications: not everything deserves to interrupt you.**

Notifications are one of the biggest attention thieves out there. They're designed to pull you back into the app, even if it's "just for a second" (which it never is). Learning to manage notifications protects focus, rest and, often, mood.

Not all notifications are bad, but many aren't urgent at all. Likes, suggested videos, "someone posted something" alerts can wait. Muting, grouping or disabling notifications doesn't mean ignoring the world, it means choosing when to engage with it.

A good rule: keep notifications only for things that really need quick attention (important messages, calls, family alerts). The phone should work for you, not boss you around every five minutes.

- **Screen time: not to spy, but to become aware.**

This feature isn't meant to monitor every minute or turn your phone into a police report. It's meant to show how much time you actually spend on each app, something most of us seriously underestimate.

Checking screen time helps spot habits, not judge them. From there, you can make small, realistic decisions: gentle limits, screen-free moments, or simply understanding what's going on. Awareness comes first; control only if it makes sense.

- **App permissions: camera, microphone, location... only when needed.**

Many apps ask for everything "just in case", and we often accept without reading. But not every app needs to know where you are, hear you, or access your camera.

Reviewing permissions regularly and asking "why does this app need this?" is a healthy habit. Removing unnecessary access isn't paranoid, it's setting digital boundaries.

- **Social media privacy: public, private and 'semi-private'.**

Public profiles are visible to anyone, including people you don't know. That's not always bad, but it requires more care.

Private profiles reduce exposure, but don't eliminate risks. Screenshots and forwards still exist.

Then there are semi-private spaces: close friends, special lists, private groups. This is where people often relax too much. One person is enough for content to leave the circle, not always through bad intentions, sometimes through carelessness.

A useful question: would I be okay if this stopped being private tomorrow? If not, it's worth thinking again.

Good settings won't fix everything, but they prevent a lot of unnecessary problems from growing bigger than they need to.

## Digital Organisation Without Losing Your Mind

A messy digital life is stressful. Very stressful. And it affects everyone: teenagers, adults and teachers alike. Chaos drains energy, distracts, and creates the constant feeling of never finishing anything.

When everything is disorganised, finding something simple becomes a mini adventure. Searching for a photo, a file or an email can take far more time than it should, and patience with it.

### *Signs of digital chaos*

If any of these sound familiar, you're not alone:

- Hundreds of screenshots you no longer remember why you saved.
- Files called "final_final_v3_now_yes", plus "final_good", "final_real" and "this_is_the_real_one".
- Emails unread since 2018, silently judging you.
- Apps installed that nobody remembers downloading.

This doesn't mean you're a messy person, it means nobody taught us how to manage digital life properly.

### *Small habits that actually help*

You don't need an extreme clean-up or a full weekend deleting files. Small habits, done gradually, work far better.

- **Use a few clear folders.** Simple systems get used. Complicated ones get abandoned.
- **Delete what no longer helps.** "Just in case" quickly becomes permanent noise.
- **Short, regular reviews.** Ten minutes occasionally beats a mythical annual clean-up.
- **Use favourites or notes for what really matters.** Don't rely on memory alone.

Organising doesn't mean controlling everything or making your phone a perfectly curated museum. It means reducing noise, saving time, and freeing mental space for better things than sorting old screenshots.

## Recommended Apps, Settings and Tips

You do not need to have 50 apps to do things properly. In fact, the more apps we collect, the more chaos we create without realising it. Every new app promises to make our lives easier, but many end up being just another thing to manage, update, learn how to use… or simply forget about until an unexpected notification appears.

Having lots of apps does not mean being more productive or more digitally advanced. Sometimes it means exactly the opposite: distraction, duplicated functions and the constant feeling that "I should be using something better". In reality, a few well-chosen and well-understood tools usually work far better than a phone full of icons that nobody remembers what they are for.

Some useful categories:

- **Password management.** To avoid always using the same password (yes, the one that starts to sweat every time you reuse it) and to stop writing them down in notes, on bits of paper or, even worse, trying to keep them all in your head and hoping nothing goes wrong.
- **Organisation and notes.** Simple apps for writing down ideas, tasks or reminders. Not to write the next great novel, but to avoid forgetting important things and to free up some mental space.
- **Time control and focus.** Tools that help you become aware of how much time you spend on certain apps and to set small limits when needed, without punishments or drama. Yes, we have mentioned this before. And yes, I will probably mention it again later. By now you should know how this works: I insist, I repeat ideas and I can be quite persistent... but it works. Sometimes you do not need a new idea, just to hear the same one a few times until, suddenly, it clicks and you actually start using it.
- **Positive content creation.** Apps that allow you to create, not just consume: editing videos, designing, writing, recording audio or preparing personal projects.

The key is not the app itself, but how and why it is used. A tool used badly makes things more complicated; a tool used well makes life simpler. Very often the problem is not the technology, but the expectations we place on it: we hope an app will organise our life, remove our stress and magically turn us into highly productive people. Spoiler: that usually does not happen.

It is not about having "the best app", the most popular one, or the one everyone recommends on social media. It is about finding the app that actually fits your needs, your age, your pace and your real habits. The best app in the world is useless if you do not use it, if it feels uncomfortable, or if it ends up being just another thing that makes you feel guilty for not making the most of it.

It is also important to understand that constantly changing tools rarely solves the problem. Jumping from app to app in search of the perfect solution usually adds more confusion than order. Sometimes the smartest choice is to use something simple, even if it is not impressive, but does its job without asking too much in return.

And if an app gives you nothing, there is absolutely nothing wrong with deleting it. Deleting is also a way of moving forward. It is not giving up or failing; it is making a conscious decision. Your phone will have less noise, your mind will feel a little lighter... and you will probably not even miss it.

## Useful Resources for Home and Classroom

This chapter would not be complete without thinking about the spaces where the most learning actually happens: home and the classroom. Because, even though the internet can feel like a wild place with no rules, the way we learn to move within it has a lot to do with what we see, talk about and practise in these two environments.

Neither at home nor in school is the goal to have all the answers, to be technology experts, or to control every step teenagers take. What really matters is accompanying them, creating spaces where making mistakes is not a drama and where digital decisions can be talked about naturally.

At home

The home is, often without us realising it, the first digital laboratory. It is where habits, attitudes and ways of reacting to online problems are learned almost by osmosis.

- Going through settings together, without drama or long speeches. Not as a surprise inspection, but as a normal routine, just like checking a school bag or tidying a room. Sharing the moment helps reduce tension and normalises the idea that settings change and need to be reviewed.
- Talking about everyday digital decisions, not only when there is a problem. Comments like "this came up on my feed", "I wasn't sure whether to share that" or "I've removed this permission" help teenagers understand that thinking before acting is normal, not a punishment.
- Normalising learning through trial and error. Making mistakes is part of the process. The important thing is not to avoid every mistake, but to learn from them without fear or embarrassment. One well-supported mistake teaches more than ten imposed rules.

At home, it is also essential to remember that example carries more weight than any lecture. The way adults use their phone, manage their time or react to fake news is also teaching, even when nothing is said explicitly.

In the classroom

The classroom is the ideal space to turn digital life into something visible, shared and reflected upon, without personalising or pointing fingers.

- Practical activities using real (or simulated) phones. Looking at settings live, comparing configurations or analysing fictional examples helps make learning concrete rather than abstract.
- Analysis of common settings. Understanding which options are switched on by default and why helps develop critical thinking and challenges the idea that "if it's set like this, it must be the best option".
- Reflection on daily digital habits. Not just which apps students use, but how they use them, when they use them and for what purpose. These conversations often raise more awareness than any list of rules.

The classroom also offers something very valuable: the chance to see that not everyone experiences digital life in the same way. Comparing experiences helps put things into perspective, reduce social pressure and understand that there is no single correct way to be on the internet.

In short, it is not about controlling every click, either at home or in school, but about teaching how to make conscious decisions, how to think before acting and how to understand that digital life, just like real life, is learned little by little, with support and without the need to do everything perfectly.

This chapter does not aim for you to do everything perfectly, but to give you real resources for a real digital world. And that, even if it does not always feel like it, is already a great deal.

# 9

# Supporting Without Controlling: Growing With Digital Independence

## Finding the balance between protection and trust

We've reached a delicate point. And yes, before we continue, I'm going to say this one last time (promise): some of the ideas in this chapter have already appeared earlier in the book. It's not a mistake, not an oversight, and not because I've run out of things to say. It's simply because this topic matters so much that it deserves to be seen from different angles… and because, let's be honest, sometimes we need to hear the same thing a few times before it really clicks.

Right. That's it. I won't repeat it again.

This chapter is about one of the hardest balances in digital education, and in education in general: how to protect without suffocating, how to support without monitoring, and how to let go gradually without disappearing completely.

Because nobody wants to be the parent or adult who controls

every click, every message and every minute of screen time. But nobody wants to look the other way and just hope everything will be fine either. Between total control and total neglect, there's a middle space. And that space is where real learning happens.

We're going to talk about parental controls without demonising them or pretending they solve everything, about rules that don't sound like punishment, about agreements that evolve over time, and about how digital responsibility is built step by step, without rushing… but without endless delays.

It's not about doing it perfectly. It's about doing it better each time, understanding that digital independence doesn't appear overnight. It's trained, supported and, little by little, trusted.

## Parental controls: why yes, how, and for how long

Parental controls tend to cause extreme reactions. For some people, they're the ultimate solution; for others, they're a kind of digital prison that destroys any sign of trust. And, as usual, the sensible truth is somewhere in the middle.

Parental controls are not the enemy, and they're not proof that we don't trust our children. They're also not a magic solution that lets us step back from real support. They're simply stabilisers. Like a bike, they make sense at the start, they help prevent serious falls… but they're not meant to stay forever.

## Why parental controls can be a good idea

At the start of digital life, teenagers (and children) don't yet have enough judgement to manage all the online risks out there. Not because they're irresponsible, but because nobody is born knowing this stuff, and the digital world is complex.

Parental controls can help to:

- **Protect from inappropriate content** when there isn't enough maturity to deal with it. This isn't about censoring the world, it's about matching access to the child's stage of life.
- **Limit screen time** while healthy habits are being built. The goal isn't to watch the clock or make the phone the enemy, but to help create balanced routines: good sleep, study, movement, a bit of boredom, and real-life social time.
- **Reduce obvious risks** without needing constant supervision. Well set up, controls can lower tension because the adult doesn't have to be "on top of it" all the time.
- **Create a clear safety framework** that communicates care, not suspicion. When explained properly, the message is: "I care about your wellbeing and I want to help you grow safely."

Used well, controls don't replace education, they support it. They're a safety net while someone learns to walk.

### *How to use them without turning it into a war*

The main mistake is rarely using parental controls, it's how they're introduced. If they appear suddenly, with no explanation or conversation, they feel like punishment or invasion. That's when conflict starts.

A few key points:

- **Explain them from the beginning.** Be clear about what they do and what they don't do.
- **Agree them whenever possible.** Not as a military order, but as shared care.
- **Match them to maturity, not just age.**
- **Review them together from time to time,** explain changes, and listen.

The underlying message should be: "It's not that I don't trust you. It's that you're still learning, and I'm here to help."

### *When they stop making sense*

This is the part adults find hardest.

Parental controls are not meant to last forever. If they never reduce, they stop educating and start controlling, and that's when they lose their value.

As teenagers show responsibility, respect rules, manage time better, and ask for help when something goes wrong, controls should:

- **be relaxed gradually;**
- **turn into agreements rather than technical blocks;**

- **make space for self-regulation and trust.**

Letting go doesn't mean disappearing. It means changing role: from guard to guide, from controller to trusted reference point.

A good sign that it's time to reduce controls isn't "never making mistakes", but being able to recognise mistakes, talk about them, and learn from them.

In short: parental controls are useful when they're used with common sense, dialogue, and an expiry date in mind. They don't educate on their own, but they can help digital independence grow with fewer knocks and more trust.

## Agreements, rules, and gradual review

If parental controls are stabilisers, then agreements and rules are the shared instruction manual. Not a 30-page legal document, just clear agreements everyone understands, remembers, and can review without needing a lawyer.

The difference between an imposed rule and an agreed pact is huge. The first is often followed out of fear or obligation; the second, when done well, is followed because it makes sense. And in digital education, that makes all the difference.

### *Why agreements work better than bans*

Absolute bans have a serious problem: they create a strong desire to break them. Especially in adolescence, when testing limits is part of growing up.

A pact, instead:

- Gives teenagers a voice and makes them feel part of the process;
- Allows adults to explain *why*, not just *what*;
- Encourages responsibility rather than blind obedience;
- Reduces conflict because rules don't appear out of nowhere.

This isn't about negotiating everything or turning every chat into an endless meeting. It's about agreeing what matters most and making it clear that rules exist to protect, not to ruin their lives.

## How to create realistic digital agreements

A good pact doesn't need to be perfect, it needs to be possible.

- **Few rules, but clear ones.** Better five well understood rules than fifteen nobody remembers.
- **Concrete rules, not vague ones.** "Don't overuse your phone" means nothing; "phones stay out of bedrooms at night" does.
- **Known consequences in advance.** Not improvised punishments in the heat of the moment.
- **Space to review and change.** What works at 12 doesn't always work at 15.

Also important: a pact isn't fixed forever, but it shouldn't be renegotiated daily either. It has a trial period, then it gets reviewed.

## Gradual review: growing up means rules change

This is one of the most important, and hardest, parts.

If a teenager keeps to the agreement, shows responsibility and manages digital life better, the rules should evolve. Keeping the exact same limits for years sends a risky message: "It doesn't matter what you do, we don't trust you more."

Gradual review means:

- adjusting time and limits as independence grows;
- replacing technical blocks with spoken agreements;
- moving from direct supervision to regular check-ins.

Not everything changes overnight. Trust is earned step by step, and it turns into more freedom… and also more responsibility.

## When a pact doesn't work

Sometimes, even with the best intentions, an agreement fails. That doesn't mean everything is ruined.

You may need to:

- Check whether the rules were realistic;
- Adjust expectations on both sides;
- Remind everyone what the pact is for;
- Temporarily return to clearer limits if needed.

The key is that mistakes don't break the dialogue. Agreements are not about proving who's in charge, they're about learning to live digitally without unnecessary drama.

In short: making agreements isn't giving up authority, it's

using it more intelligently. Rules that are explained, agreed and reviewed teach far more than rules that are simply imposed.

## This bit is for you, teenager

Right, let's be direct. This part is just for you.

When your parents or the adults you live with talk about agreements, rules and reviews, they're usually not trying to ruin your digital life or take away fun for no reason. Most of the time, they're trying to do something quite hard: keep you safe in a world that moves fast and that they don't fully control either.

A pact doesn't mean they don't trust you. In fact, it often means the opposite. It means they believe you can give an opinion, make decisions, and take some responsibility. If they trusted you *zero*, there wouldn't be pacts, there would be orders, full stop.

Clear rules save you problems, even if it doesn't feel like it right now. Knowing what's expected, what the limits are, and what happens if they're broken prevents endless arguments and random punishments. And yes, some rules can feel over the top... but most of them come from fear that something will go wrong, not from a desire to control you.

Gradual review matters for you. Every time you keep an agreement, manage your time better, or speak up when something is getting out of hand, you're sending a strong message: "I can handle this." Over time, that message often turns into more freedom.

Also: asking for changes calmly works much better than demanding them angrily. Explain how you feel, what you'd like to change, and why you think you're ready. That opens more doors than shouting ever will.

In short: agreements aren't a cage, they're training. They're not there to stop you, but to help you reach the point where they're no longer needed. And the sooner you show you can manage digital life sensibly, the sooner the stabilisers start to come off.

## Learning to let go without disappearing

This is probably one of the hardest parts of digital support. Not because adults don't care, but because letting go feels scary. Especially when what's at stake is someone you love, in an online world that isn't always easy to understand.

Letting go doesn't mean stopping caring, looking away, or saying "they'll figure it out." It means changing how you're present: moving from constant control to available support, from monitoring to guided trust.

For many adults, letting go feels like irresponsibility. But it's actually the opposite: it's a conscious educational decision. Nobody learns independence if they never get space to make their own choices... and to make a few mistakes.

### *Being close without being on top of them*

Supporting without controlling means being there, but not invading. Being available without being constantly present. Knowing enough to spot warning signs, but not turning every digital action into an interrogation.

Being close doesn't mean knowing everything, checking every message, or reading every conversation. It means creating the kind of relationship where a teenager knows they can come to you if something feels uncomfortable, worrying, or out of control. And, oddly enough, that usually happens more easily when they don't feel watched all the time.

Practical ways to find the balance:

- **Show interest without spying.** Ask what apps they're using, what they like watching or creating, what trends they're into, not to police them, but to understand their world.
- **Listen more than you talk.** Often, the biggest support isn't quick advice, but giving them space to explain in their own words.
- **Talk about digital life when things are fine too.** If the phone only becomes a topic during conflict, the message is "the internet equals problems."
- **Accept they won't tell you everything.** That's not educational failure, it's part of growing up. The goal isn't knowing everything; it's knowing they *could* tell you if they needed to.

This isn't a comfortable position. It takes patience, self-control, and accepting some uncertainty. But that space is exactly where trust is built and digital independence starts to grow.

### *Trust isn't closing your eyes*

Letting go isn't stepping away. Trust isn't blind. It isn't "do whatever you want and we'll see." Trust is active: it's built, reviewed and adjusted.

Trust means observing without invading, supporting without suffocating, and being available if something goes wrong.

It doesn't mean ignoring signs or pretending everything is perfect because it's easier.

In practice, trust means:

- Believing a teenager *can* make good choices, even if they don't always do it;
- Accepting mistakes as part of learning (small, medium, and the occasional one that becomes a future awkward story);
- Knowing that if things get complicated, there will be space for a real conversation, not a trial, not an interrogation.

When an adult shows trust, they also send a powerful message: "I trust you, even when you mess up." That message often teaches more than any rule, punishment, or hidden control app ever could.

Trust doesn't remove risk, but it creates something far more valuable long-term: a relationship where a teenager can fail, learn and try again without fear of losing the adult's support.

### *When letting go is hard (because it usually is)*

Let's be honest: letting go is difficult. Sometimes very difficult. And that's normal. After years of protecting, anticipating problems and trying to keep things safe, it makes sense to feel nervous.

Behind that difficulty are real fears: online risks, bad influences, not finding out in time, consequences that can't be undone. These fears are understandable and common. Naming them doesn't make anyone a worse parent or educator, it makes them human and responsible.

The problem starts when fear becomes constant control.

When fear is in charge, protection can feel like distrust, even if that's not the intention. That's why it helps to bring those fears into the open and talk about them calmly.

Saying things like "This worries me," "I don't always know the best way to do this," or "I'm learning with you" often opens more doors than strict orders or silent control ever will. Showing vulnerability doesn't weaken authority, it often makes it more believable.

### *Letting go also teaches*

Every small space of independence is a real learning opportunity. Choosing when to use the phone, deciding what to share, handling conflict, asking for help, making mistakes and owning them, these skills only develop if there's room to practise.

If everything is always decided and corrected from outside, learning stays shallow. People obey, but they don't internalise. That's why letting go, even when uncomfortable, is essential.

Little by little, letting go teaches responsibility, judgement and self-control, but also confidence. When a teenager gets space, they understand something is expected of them, and that often creates more maturity than rigid rules.

Independence doesn't switch on overnight. It's more like a staircase: sometimes you go up a step, sometimes you slip back half a step, sometimes you need to pause. Letting go allows that process to happen naturally, without unrealistic pressure.

Over time, it also changes the adult's role: from directing every step to observing, guiding and supporting when needed. The adult doesn't disappear, they just stop filling all the space.

In the end, learning to let go isn't losing influence. It's changing it. It's moving from controlling every move to becoming a safe reference point, the person they can come to when things get confusing, uncomfortable, or difficult. And that shift, even if it's hard, is one of the biggest successes of good digital support.

## Digital responsibility, step by step

Digital responsibility doesn't suddenly appear, as if one morning a teenager wakes up and says: "Today I know how to use the internet perfectly." If only. Responsibility is built slowly, through experience, mistakes, support, and those uncomfortable-but-necessary conversations.

Thinking of it as a step-by-step process helps both parents and teenagers because it reduces pressure. It's not about getting it all right from the start, it's about improving over time.

### *Step 1: understand that everything has consequences*

Every digital action leaves a trace, has an impact, and can have effects that aren't immediate.

For teenagers: not everything that happens online stays online. A comment, photo or angry message can travel further than you expect. That's not meant to scare you, it's meant to remind you that digital life is real life.

For adults: repeating this calmly works better than turning every mistake into a tragedy.

### *Step 2: learn to decide before posting*

A key skill: pause for one second. Just one second. It sounds easy on paper. In real life, with emotions and pressure, it isn't.

Simple questions help more than long speeches:

- Would I post this if I knew more people would see it?
- Will I feel comfortable with this later?
- Am I posting because I want to, or because I want a reaction?

### *Step 3: manage mistakes without hiding them*

Mistakes will happen. To everyone.

The key isn't avoiding them at all costs, but what you do when they appear:

- Acknowledge them;
- Talk about them;
- Fix what you can;
- Learn something for next time.

For teenagers, asking for help when something is out of control is maturity, not weakness.

For adults, calm reactions make it far more likely teenagers will ask for help again in the future.

### *Step 4: gain independence gradually*

Responsibility grows as trust grows. More freedom doesn't arrive automatically, and it isn't granted just because someone has a birthday. It comes when someone shows judgement, consistency and the ability to handle small decisions without turning everything into chaos.

In real terms, this often looks like:

- Fewer technical controls and more spoken agreements;
- More choice over time and content;
- More responsibility for decisions and consequences.

This isn't a gift. It's the logical outcome of the learning process: when someone shows they can handle more freedom, it makes sense to give it. And if they're not ready yet, slowing down is fine.

For teenagers, it's a chance to prove they can handle it. For adults, it's an exercise in trust, patience, and sometimes biting your tongue. But done well, it changes the relationship: less control, more dialogue, and a shared sense of real growth.

### *Step 5: know when to ask for help*

Being digitally responsible doesn't mean doing everything alone. In fact, trying to handle everything solo is a quick route to unnecessary trouble.

In a world that changes quickly and can be confusing, asking for help is a skill, not weakness. Saying "I'm not sure," "This makes me uncomfortable," or "I need help with this" is often smarter than pretending everything is fine.

Adults and teenagers are on the same team. Not opponents. Digital responsibility isn't suffering in silence or fixing everything alone, it's knowing when to rely on others and who you can trust.

For teenagers, asking for help early can stop a small problem becoming huge. For adults, responding calmly and without blame makes it far more likely teenagers will come again.

## And from the classroom: what can teachers do?

Although this chapter is mainly aimed at families and teenagers, teachers also play a key role in finding this balance. And no, teachers don't need to be experts in tech, social media, or the latest app to help. Often, the most useful thing isn't knowing more, it's being present in the right way.

Practical ideas from the classroom:

- **Normalise digital doubts.** When a student brings up an awkward online situation, you don't need the perfect answer. "That's not simple," "Let's think about it together," or "This could happen to anyone" reduces shame and opens space for dialogue.
- **Encourage reflection, not control.** School isn't the place to spy on students' personal digital lives, but it is the place to discuss scenarios, questions and dilemmas that encourage thinking before acting. Education is not surveillance.
- **Reinforce the idea of asking for help.** Remind students clearly that speaking to a trusted adult when something online feels wrong isn't "snitching" or overreacting, it's self-care. Teachers can be one of those accessible adults.

- **Work with families when needed.** Not to panic or accuse, but to support. When school and home pull in the same direction, the message is much clearer.
- **Model digital consistency.** How teachers speak online, handle conflict, and respond to mistakes sets an example, even without meaning to.

Teachers don't need to control students' digital lives. Their role is to offer context, calm and judgement. Sometimes being the adult who listens without judgement is already a huge help, and yes, that teaches too.

## A final reminder (for everyone)

Digital responsibility isn't measured by never making mistakes, but by how mistakes are handled, talked about and learned from. Mistakes are part of the process, online and offline.

Being responsible online doesn't mean being perfect. It means being aware: aware that online decisions matter, that they have impact, and that there's always room to improve. It also means being flexible: what works today may need adjusting tomorrow, and growing up means reviewing habits and rules without drama.

Digital independence doesn't arrive overnight, wrapped up like a present. It's built slowly, conversation by conversation, experience by experience, and yes, mistake by mistake... match by match, as a certain Atlético Madrid manager would say at the time of writing. Sometimes you move forward clearly; sometimes you take a small step back that teaches more than you realise at the time.

When support is based on trust, dialogue and availability, not only control, independence stops feeling frightening. It starts to make sense, becomes manageable, and over time becomes a powerful tool for moving through the digital world with judgement, confidence, and a bit more shared calm.

# 10

# Looking Ahead: Technology, Identity and People

## Closing the circle with an optimistic and realistic view

We've reached the last chapter. And yes, this is that moment when you look back at everything you've covered, take a deep breath and think: "Right… after all of this, what now?" Because talking about technology, digital identity, risks, rules and support is all well and good, but the real question is how all of this fits into the future that is already here.

This chapter doesn't aim to give final answers or magic formulas, just like the rest of the book. They don't exist. What it does try to do is close the circle with a clear idea: technology is not the problem, and it's not the solution to everything either. It's part of the world we live in, whether we like it or not, and learning to live with it in a healthy way is a shared task.

We'll talk about why the internet isn't the enemy, why educating for a connected world makes more sense than trying to switch it off, the importance of thinking and choosing with good judgement and, above all, something we sometimes forget in the middle of screens and algorithms: being a good person still matters... online too.

This isn't a chapter to scare you, or to idealise the future as if everything will be wonderful. It's an invitation to look ahead with realism, confidence and a bit of hope. Because the digital future is not only about technology, it's about people.

## The internet isn't the enemy

Sometimes we talk about the internet as if it were a film villain: dark, dangerous, always lurking, with creepy background music and everything. But the reality is much less dramatic and much more everyday. The internet isn't good or bad by itself. It's a huge, powerful tool full of possibilities... and like any tool, it depends on how it's used, who uses it and why.

Wonderful things happen online every day: people learn, create, meet people they would never have met otherwise, share ideas, discover passions and build amazing projects from an ordinary bedroom. People also ask for help, find communities and feel less alone when the offline world isn't enough. That is the internet too, even if it doesn't always make headlines.

Of course, unpleasant things happen as well. There are conflicts, abuse, misinformation and situations nobody wants to experience. But that doesn't make the internet "the enemy", in the same way a city doesn't become unliveable just because it has risks. The key isn't escaping the environment, it's learning how to move through it with good judgement, like we do in any other part of life.

Education isn't about teaching fear of the internet. It's about learning to understand it. Fear freezes people, creates rejection and kills conversation. Knowledge, on the other hand, protects, gives tools and helps people make better choices. When everything is framed through fear, the digital world becomes a forbidden topic; when it's framed through understanding, it becomes an educational opportunity.

For teenagers, this is key: the internet isn't designed to hurt you, but it's not designed to look after you either. It's not a parent, a teacher or a friend who is watching out for you. It's an environment. And moving well in an environment takes attention, judgement and a bit of learning through trial and error. Knowing this doesn't reduce your freedom, it makes it safer.

For adults, the challenge is to stop seeing the internet as one single, threatening block and start noticing contexts, uses and possibilities. Creating isn't the same as consuming. Sharing isn't the same as watching. Learning isn't the same as being dragged along. The more nuanced an adult's view is, the easier it is to support without drama.

When we stop demonising technology, conversations become much easier. And, interestingly, more effective. Because speaking about something without fear helps us listen better, explain better and educate better in a world that is not going to disconnect, no matter how tempting it sometimes is to switch off the router and pretend none of this exists.

## Educating for a world that isn't going to disconnect

Here's an uncomfortable but necessary truth: the internet isn't going to switch off. It won't disappear, it won't magically shrink, and it won't stay only for responsible adults who read the terms and conditions properly and accept cookies with full awareness. It's here to stay, and it will keep evolving, whether we like it or not, at a speed that usually runs ahead of our ability to adapt.

So education today can't be based on "they'll learn when they're older" or "it's just a phase". Digital life is part of real life from a very young age, and learning to live with it matters as much as learning to cross a road, manage money or understand that not everything that shines is gold. The digital world isn't an optional extra, it's one of the main places where relationships, identity and experiences are built.

Educating for a connected world means accepting a few realities that aren't always comfortable, but are necessary:

- Teenagers will have digital experiences that adults won't fully control, even if we'd love to have a complete map.
- There will be mistakes, misunderstandings and awkward situations, because learning always includes getting things wrong.
- Progress won't be neat or perfect: there will be steps forward, steps back and moments of shared frustration.

Accepting that doesn't mean giving up or looking away. It means changing the goal. Instead of aiming for total control (which is usually impossible), the aim becomes supporting, guiding and giving tools so that, little by little, each person can make better decisions for themselves.

Trying to disconnect someone from the digital world as an "education strategy" usually creates more problems than it solves. It can cause emotional distance, encourage secrecy and break the dialogue. Teaching people to connect *better*, on the other hand, opens the door to independence, judgement and responsibility. It doesn't remove risk, but it prepares people to face it with more calm, more awareness and more resources.

## Thinking, choosing and creating with judgement

One of the biggest challenges of the digital future isn't technical, it's mental. We live surrounded by constant stimuli, instant opinions, endless content and decisions that feel urgent even when they almost never are. Everything moves fast, very fast, and thinking before acting has become almost a rebellious act. In a world that pushes reaction, pausing to reflect is almost a superpower.

Developing digital judgement means learning to stop for a second before clicking, sharing or replying. Not to live in fear or permanent suspicion, but to understand what's happening around you and decide with a bit more head and a bit less impulse.

Little by little, digital judgement means learning to:

- Not believe everything you see or read, even if it comes with lots of likes or a very convincing headline.
- Understand why something appears on your screen: who made it, with what intention, and why the algorithm decided to show it to you.
- Choose what you consume and what you don't, accepting that not everything deserves your time, attention or energy.
- Decide when to engage and when to move on, without feeling you always have to comment, reply or be present.

For teenagers, that's a big shift: moving from impulsive reactions (because something annoys you, entertains you or provokes you) to consciously choosing what to do with it. It isn't easy, and nobody is born knowing how. It takes practice, mistakes and plenty of internal conversations like "Is this worth it?" or "Does this show a good side of me?"

For adults, developing judgement means accepting something less comfortable: judgement can't be forced by decree. You can't install it with one serious talk or one rule written in capital letters. Judgement is trained. Sometimes through calm conversations, sometimes through modelling, and sometimes by allowing someone to mess up a little and learn from it, even when it's hard, even when it's scary.

Creating with judgement is the next natural step. It's not only about consuming what others make, but adding something of your own to the digital world: an idea, a project, a reflection, content that says something about who you are and how you think. Creating forces you to slow down, structure ideas and think about impact.

It also helps you understand the digital world better. When you stop being only a spectator and become a creator, you gain perspective: you understand platforms better, why some things spread and others don't, and how messages are built. All of that strengthens judgement and supports a more solid, coherent and genuine digital identity.

Thinking, choosing and creating with judgement doesn't mean doing everything perfectly. It means doing it with intention. And in a digital world that constantly pushes automatic reaction, that is already a huge step forward.

## Being a good person matters online too

It sounds obvious, almost like basic "how to live with others" advice, but we don't always apply it: the core rules of being a good person don't switch off when you turn on a screen. Respect, empathy, responsibility and care for others don't depend on the medium, even if the internet sometimes makes us feel like they do. There is no "airplane mode" for values.

Online, where we can't see someone's face, hear their tone of voice, or read body language, it's easy to forget that there's a real person on the other side. Someone with emotions, a good day or a bad one, insecurities, context. Being a good person online means not forgetting that, especially when it would be easiest to forget.

Being a good person on the internet doesn't mean being perfect or always saying the "right" thing. It means using the same judgement we would use face to face, with a bit more care, because the impact can be bigger and can last longer. In practice, that often looks like:

- Thinking about how your words might affect someone before you send them, especially when you're angry.
- Not joining in with mocking, humiliation or attacks, even if they feel normal, get likes, or look like "just a joke".
- Knowing when to stop when a conversation brings nothing good and only creates noise and tension.
- Owning mistakes and apologising when needed, harder online, but often worth even more.

For teenagers, this means understanding something simple but important: digital distance doesn't remove emotional responsibility. Just because you can't see someone's reaction doesn't mean it doesn't exist. A comment, a shared laugh, or even staying silent can affect others more than you think. Understanding that isn't a limitation, it's maturity.

For parents and teachers, this matters for one very clear reason: example teaches more than any speech. Teenagers don't only listen to what we say; they watch how we comment on news, how we reply to someone who thinks differently, how we talk about others online or in messaging groups. And yes, how we manage our own digital mistakes.

If an adult talks about respect but writes aggressive comments, shares cruel messages or mocks others online, the real lesson is not the one they think they're teaching. But when an adult shows self-control, empathy and the ability to correct themselves, even publicly, they teach a powerful lesson without needing many words.

Being a good person online and offline aren't two different things. It's the same thing in different settings. Digital identity isn't only built through what you post, but through how you interact, how you respond and how you treat others. And all of that leaves a trace.

In a world that's more connected every year, teaching technology without teaching values isn't enough. And teaching values without applying them online isn't enough either.

## Looking ahead without fear

Looking ahead in the digital world isn't about controlling everything, knowing everything, or avoiding every risk as if life came with a laminated instruction manual. It's more about accepting a truth that is uncomfortable but also freeing: we can't control everything, and that's okay.

The digital future isn't a surprise test you have to pass with top marks. It's a long road, full of small decisions, continuous learning and the occasional stumble. And, by the way, stumbles are part of learning online and offline, even if we don't always like admitting it.

Technology will keep changing. A lot. When we think we finally understand one platform, another one appears. When we finally get used to an app, it updates and the button we used yesterday has vanished. And when we think "this can't possibly get faster", the internet laughs and speeds up again. That's how it works.

But in the middle of all that constant change, something stays surprisingly stable: people. Their needs, their fears, their need to belong, to express themselves, to be seen and heard. That's why, even if platforms change, the values that help us move through them are the same: dialogue, trust, judgement, empathy and humanity.

Looking ahead without fear doesn't mean looking ahead without caution. It means not living permanently on high alert. It means understanding that digital education isn't about building higher and higher walls, it's about building stronger bridges. Bridges that allow people to talk, ask, make mistakes and learn without everything becoming a dramatic family crisis.

For teenagers, this matters: nobody expects you to do everything perfectly. Nobody does. What's expected is that you learn, that you ask questions when something doesn't feel right, and that you remember that even if adults sometimes look like they don't understand anything, they are usually trying to help... even if their aim isn't always perfect.

For parents and teachers, looking ahead calmly means accepting that educating today is more complex than ever, and also more necessary than ever. It means trusting a bit more, listening a bit better, and understanding that supporting doesn't mean watching every step. It means being available when it matters. Even when it's hard. Even when it's scary. Even when we feel like switching off the Wi-Fi and moving to a mountain.

Realistic optimism isn't believing everything will be fine automatically. It's knowing we have tools, experience, past conversations and relationships strong enough to deal with what comes with a bit more calm. And in a hyper-connected world, that's already a big advantage.

This chapter isn't meant to "close" anything in a final way. Quite the opposite, it leaves things open on purpose. Because digital education isn't completed, finished, or filed away in a neatly named folder. It adapts, it gets reviewed, it gets discussed... and it gets lived. Day by day. With screens. And, thankfully, without them too.

# 11

# What still matters is the same

At this point, the usual thing would be to close the book with a big, brilliant conclusion, an epic line, or a "mission accomplished" feeling. But the reality is different, much simpler, and maybe that's why it feels more honest.

If you've made it this far, you've probably done it with doubts, questions, and that very familiar feeling of "Am I doing this right?". And it's worth saying this from the start: that doubt isn't a problem. It's a very clear sign that you care. And when you care, you're already doing much more than you think.

Throughout these pages we've talked about digital footprints, identity, risks, mistakes, awkward conversations, controls, rules, agreements and the future. We've repeated ideas (yes, some more than once, because I can be a bit relentless, and because important things usually need repeating). But underneath it all, everything comes back to something very simple: people trying to look after other people in a world that's more connected every day.

There isn't a perfect family or perfect teachers. And there

isn't a teenager who always makes the right decisions, thinks before posting, and checks privacy settings with real enthusiasm. And that's fine. Learning has always been imperfect, full of trial and error, clumsy conversations, and silences that arrive before the words.

Digital education isn't about having all the answers. It's about being available. Listening even when we don't fully understand. Saying "I don't know, but let's look at it together." Making mistakes, putting them right, and trying again. And yes, sometimes it's also about taking a deep breath before reacting... which we don't always manage perfectly either.

Technology isn't going to disappear. Screens will still be there. Platforms will change, trends will come and go, and algorithms will do their thing. But one thing doesn't change: the need to feel supported, understood and respected. That is still the centre of it all, online too.

Maybe the biggest lesson here isn't how to set up an app or spot one specific risk. Maybe it's understanding that supporting doesn't mean controlling, and trusting doesn't mean leaving someone to it. It means walking alongside them, even when the pace doesn't match, and even when you feel like switching off the router and pretending it's 1995.

If you're a parent or a teacher, remember this: your example matters more than you realise. Not because you're perfect, but because you're consistent, human, and able to admit mistakes. And if you're a teenager reading this (yes, you), here's something important: when adults worry, it's almost never to make your life difficult. Most of the time it's because they want to help... even if they don't always know how to do it without making a bit of a mess.

This book isn't trying to end any debate or offer final answers. It's aiming for something much more modest, and, at the same time, more necessary: to encourage us to think, to talk, and to support each other with a bit more calm and a bit less fear.

Because in the end, with all the technology, screens and constant change, what matters most is still what it has always been: people looking after people. And thankfully, there's still no algorithm that can replace that.

www.ingramcontent.com/pod-product-compliance
Lightning Source LLC
LaVergne TN
LVHW100311210926
848480LV00003B/1097